Tl

Jack Altman

JPMGUIDES

Contents

Maps

Fold-out map

This Way the Rhine

Old Father Rhine

The mighty Rhine lies at the heart of western European civilization. It is steeped in the history of the four countries through which it flows—Switzerland, France, Germany and The Netherlands. Taking its source from two small Alpine headstreams in eastern Switzerland's St Gotthard massif, it heads west and north for over 1,390 km (868 miles) to its delta on the Dutch coast of the North Sea. It is by no means Europe's longest river—Russia and Eastern Europe have ten that are longer and the Danube is twice as long—but none has so many great old cities along its banks. Starting out from Amsterdam, a cruise upstream towards Switzerland passes through Düsseldorf, Cologne, Bonn, Koblenz, Mainz, Worms, Strasbourg and Basle, most tracing their history back to Roman times. Along the way are the romantic towers of medieval castles, majestic cathedral spires, eerie cliffs or sunny vineyards. Side trips along the tributaries pass through the cheerful Mosel wine-country of Cochem and Bernkastel-Kues to Trier on the Luxembourg border, along the Main river past the great banking centre of Frankfurt and Aschaffenburg to Würzburg (more great wine-country), or up the Neckar to historic Heidelberg.

Heading South

The stretch of the river between Amsterdam and Koblenz has witnessed the passage of many invaders—from the Roman legions garrisoned here by Julius Caesar to fight off the Germanic "barbarians", to the Allied armies establishing bridgeheads to cross the Rhine in World War II. You float past towns that have rebuilt their medieval churches after the wartime destruction, through the mighty Ruhr district at Duisburg. Düsseldorf, the Ruhr's administrative centre and capital of the state of North Rhine-Westphalia, is a gleaming centre of fashion and the fine arts.

Cologne stands out as the region's majestic cathedral town, boasting splendid museums of medieval, Renaissance and modern art—and sharing with Düsseldorf the reputation for the most spectacular Mardi Gras carnival festivities. Long a commercial and cultural centre, Cologne has witnessed the nation's growth from earliest Roman times to its present state of comfortable stability. Its site on the Rhine is of

As you approach St Goarshausen, you may hear the song of the Lorelei.

prime importance. The old city was founded on the left bank, the new industrial centre (Deutz) on the right. It is the ideal starting place for a visit to the Rhine Valley, land of every poetic image dear to the romantic side of the German character. But it is also a place of coal barges, express trains and juggernaut lorries, cement works and power plants.

Presiding over the fortunes of West Germany's postwar Federal Republic, Bonn proved a worthy capital, and now it resumes with greater vigour its traditional role as a cultural centre, the birthplace of Beethoven. And where better to taste and compare wines than Koblenz, looking west to the vineyards of the Mosel and south to those of the Rhine Valley?

The Stuff of Dreams

Germany indulges its most beguiling dreams floating through the Rhine Valley. This is the land of the Nibelung saga's dwarfs, river maidens and darker heroes, of the enticing siren Lorelei, and of fairytale castle ruins atop soaring crags shrouded in mist. But it's also a land of smiling vineyards, elegant avenues of poplars and gardens full of flowers. In the cheery colourful villages, the quaint half-timbered gingerbread houses look good enough to eat.

Even if you can't nibble at the walls and windowsills, many of the houses have been turned into heavenly pastry shops, or taverns. Rhinelanders have a healthy appetite for the good life.

But it is the small villages that give the Rhine Valley its distinctive character. If Rüdesheim is the best known of the wine villages, Bacharach may be the prettiest, while Boppard and Lorch can make equal claims to the highest quality in the Rhine's white wines, each with attractive castles and churches. Assmannshausen boasts a potent red wine and hot springs that have cured aches and pains since Roman times. Bingen is famous both for its wines and for its legendary bishop devoured in a dungeon in the middle of the river. And don't let anybody tell you these legends are not true. By the time you reach St Goarshausen for your first glimpse of the Lorelei rock, we promise you will see the golden-haired maiden, or at least hear her song.

White Wines and Russet-Hued Cathedrals

On the southern stretch of the navigable part of the Rhine, the river passes through Switzerland, France and Germany. Whereas, north of Mainz, castle battlements dominate the skyline, along this stretch the horizon is punctuated by the graceful spires of Romanesque and Gothic cathedrals. The churches here, most notably in the venerable towns of Worms and Speyer, are built of the distinctively reddish limestone quarried in the Palatinate. From the port-city of Mannheim, an important cultural centre, a side-trip along the Neckar reveals the most illustrious of castle ruins—the great residence of the Palatinate princes at Heidelberg.

A recurring battlefield for three centuries of devastating wars between France and Germany, Strasbourg is today a resolutely European city, the seat of the Council of Europe and the Parliament of the European Union.

Up in the northwest corner of Switzerland, Basle (Basel in German and Bâle in French) looks across two international frontiers, with France to the west of the Rhine and Germany to the east. Basle has prospered from its location astride the Rhine at the point where the navigable stretch of the river begins. In the Middle Ages, it was a vital crossroads for the exchange of goods between the Mediterranean and the North Sea and between Swabia and Burgundy, while promoting its own thriving silk manufacturing. Basle has switched its activities to chemicals, pharmaceuticals and high finance, but it continues to ship Swiss exports to the sea.

5

Flashback

Beginnings

For palaeontologists seeking the fossils and bones of human pre-history, the Rhineland is truly the cradle of mankind in Germany. From a jawbone and teeth found in a sandpit just east of the Rhine in the Neckar Valley, scientists deduce that a *Homo heidelbergensis* eked out a living here some 400,000 years ago. Germany's earliest attested humanoid ranks as a *Homo erectus*, but not yet *sapiens*. Fossiles found nearby suggest he hunted mammoth, rhinoceros and elk when the Rhineland climate was much warmer. The 50,000-year-old cranium of the famous Neanderthal Man was dug up by railway workers in 1856 in a cave in the Neander Valley near Düsseldorf. He was a real *Homo sapiens*, albeit a subspecies generally considered not to be a direct ancestor of modern man—an uncle rather than a father. A Cro-Magnon couple, hunters and fruit-gatherers, were active in the Bonn-Oberkassel region 10,000 years ago. Found together with the human remains

Remains of the Barbara Baths at Trier on the Mosel—the first Roman garrison in the region.

were small carved bone figurines suggesting some kind of early religious observance.

From around 750 BC, Celts prospering from their skill with iron tools and weapons settled on the west bank of the Rhine. The river's name is of Celtic origin, meaning "current" to which the Celts attributed spiritual qualities as a guardian of chastity and domestic virtue. The east bank was occupied by tribes the Celts called Germanic, meaning "neighbours".

Roman Empire

The Germanic king Ariovistus crossed the Rhine in 72 BC with 15,000 troops, conquering the part of Gaul now known as Alsace and the Palatinate (Rheinland-Pfalz). In response to a Gallic call for help, Julis Caesar defeated Ariovistus in 58 BC and drove the Germanic tribes back across the river. The Gallic left bank was declared a Roman protectorate. To keep out Germanic tribes, the region's first garrison of Roman legions was set up on the Mosel at Trier (Augusta Treverorum, 16 BC), followed on the Rhine by Xanten (Vetera Castra 15 BC) and Koblenz (Confluentia, confluence, of Mosel and Rhine, 9 BC). Cologne had been founded earlier in 38 BC, when Augustus's general Agrippa brought a Germanic tribe, the Ubii, across to the left bank to establish the town of Oppidum Ubiorum. (It was Julia Agrippina, wife and murderess of the Roman Emperor Claudius, who renamed her birthplace Colonia Claudia Ara Agrippinensis, shortened later to Colonia.)

Roman conquest of Germany stopped at the Rhine after defeat by Arminius—Hermann to the Germans—in the battle of Teutoburger Forest, AD 9. The Roman Empire set up its frontier (*limes*) along the river's right bank—an embankment, dry moat and palisades fortified by towers every 16 km (10 miles), starting just opposite Andernach and continuing east on the Taunus ridge along the Main river. Rome's Rhineland was divided into two provinces, with Mainz (Castrum Moguntiacum) as capital of Upper Germania and Cologne as capital of Lower Germania.

Trier prospered as a commercial centre, attracting merchants from Greece and Italy. Syrian missionary Eucharius brought Christianity to Mosel Valley in AD 72 and Romans introduced wine-growing. Trier became capital of Belgica Prima province in 117. Constantine the Great made it his imperial residence (306– 312), when it was known as Roma Secunda. Trier's Agritius of Antioch was Germany's first bishop (314).

Barbarians and Christians

From the 4th century, the "barbarians" began their devastating invasions of the Roman Rhineland, first the Alemanni, who conquered Mainz and Cologne, later the Burgundians, who were in turn defeated by the Huns. Turmoil continued with wars between the Alemanni and the Franks. The latter achieved supremacy under Clovis, who spread Christianity through the Rhineland. In 742, the Roman Church made Mainz the ecclesiastical capital of Germany.

Strasbourg, originally the Roman garrison of Argentoratum, was destroyed by the Huns in 451 and rebuilt by the Franks as Strateburgum ("city of roadways"), the name first mentioned by 6th-century historian Gregory of Tours. It became a crossroads of French and German cultures, highlighted in 842 by the Strasbourg Oath of Alliance between the Carolingian armies of Louis II and Karl II, written, for first time, in both French and German. In 923 the town was incorporated into the German Empire and ruled by bishops.

At the beginning of the 9th century, Charlemagne had established a Christian European empire with his imperial palace on the edge of the Rhineland at Aachen. In Charlemagne's grandsons' carve-up of the empire (843), Ludwig "the German" took Frankfurt for the capital of his new, German-speaking kingdom. Basle, a bishopric since the 7th century, was annexed by Burgundy in 912 and incorporated into the German Empire in 1033.

Middle Ages

From 1092 to 1212, Crusaders started out from the Rhineland with a wave of bloody pogroms against the Jewish communities in Speyer, Worms, Mainz, Rüdesheim and Cologne. By the 12th century, a golden age for the Rhineland, the archbishops of Mainz, Cologne and Trier became the most powerful princes in the German Empire. Named Aurea Moguntia (Golden Mainz) by Emperor Frederick Barbarossa in 1184, the city shared only with Rome the title of Holy See. Speyer and Worms were honoured as the seats of imperial legislative assemblies (diets). In the 11th and 12th centuries, Romanesque architecture blossomed in the churches of Speyer, Mainz and Worms, followed in the 13th by the great Gothic cathedral of Strasbourg.

Trade boomed. Forty years after beginning the building of its cathedral (1248), Cologne was prospering as a member of the Hanseatic League, trading with Bruges and London. Things in Trier looked more cheerful when wine-growing was revived in the Mosel. Frankfurt's first charter for an annual summer fair was awarded in 1240. In 1356, the great business centre on the Main was made the seat of the election of German (i.e. Holy Roman) Emperors by appointed electors and declared in 1372 a free imperial city with independent status.

Koblenz had its first hour of glory when Emperor Ludwig von Bayern held his Reichstag assembly there in 1338, defying papal authority, and made King Edward of England his (short-lived) deputy for the empire west of the Rhine. In 1343 the town's powerful archbishop Balduin built a bridge over the Mosel—the sturdy Balduinbrücke which withstood all wars and revolutions until it was bombed in 1945.

The great catastrophe of the 14th century came with the Black Death—by lung disease—of 1348. It decimated the Rhineland population and was accompanied by new pogroms against Jews accused of poisoning the wells.

Reformation and Renaissance

The 15th and 16th centuries were marked by great movements in art and religion. Rhenish painting

Cologne, detail of a German woodcut dating from 1493.

rose to prominence with its so-called "soft style" *(weicher Stil)* in which Cologne's Stephan Lochner (1410–52) was the outstanding master. Martin Schongauer (1450–91) introduced a more vigorous manner to his painting for the *Last Judgment* fresco in Breisach Cathedral. In 1515 Matthias Grünewald painted his great altarpiece for the Isenheim monastery, now part of Colmar in Alsace.

In the 1450s Johann Gutenberg built his first printing press in Strasbourg and took it home to Mainz. Permitting the mass publication of Martin Luther's Reformation sermons, the printing press became a major factor in launching the Protestant movement throughout Europe.

At the Diet of Worms in 1521, Luther was outlawed by Emperor Charles V. The monk's attack on the custom of the faithful buying indulgences to dodge purgatory was a direct, if unwitting threat to his German superior, the Archbishop of Mainz. To raise extra money for the rebuilding of St Peter's, the pope had announced a special jubilee indulgence with which sinners could buy a way out of purgatory not just for themselves but also for relatives who had neglected to pay up before they died. Sharing 50/50 with the pope, the Archbishop of Mainz needed the revenues from these new indulgences to reimburse the great Fugger banking family for a loan with which he had bought the archbishopric in the first place.

The protestation of the Lutheran princes in Speyer gave rise to the name of the Protestants in 1529. The Rhineland largely resisted the Reformation, but Strasbourg, Heidelberg and Basle became strong Protestant bastions. In 1544, Jesuits spearheaded the Counter-Reformation with schools in Cologne, seat of the papal nuncio for Germany from 1584.

Meanwhile, Alsace came increasingly under French influence during France's Wars of Religion at the end of the 16th century.

Thirty Years' War

The Thirty Years' War (1618–48) devastated the Rhineland and the Palatinate. Originally a religious war between the Catholic League and the Protestant Union, it soon involved all the major European powers—Spain, Sweden and France as well as all the German and Austrian princes—viciously defending their political and economic rather than religious interests. Typical of the nationwide catastrophe, Bacharach was besieged or captured eight times and the people were reduced to eating grass. For centuries after in rural Rhineland communities, parents have threatened their naughty children with the words: "Die Schweden kommen!" ("The Swedes are coming!").

After the 1648 Peace of Westphalia, Alsace became an informal French protectorate. Louis XIV established full control when his armies occupied Strasbourg in 1681. Pro-French Catholic bishops facilitated the conquest and even the Protestants, spared the persecution of French Huguenots, barely objected to the annexation which followed in 1697.

In 1689 and 1693, as part of Louis XIV's scorched-earth strategy against Habsburg armies, French troops under the ruthless command of François Louvois burned over 100 towns in the Rhineland. They included Boppard, Bingen, Mainz, Oppenheim, Speyer, Worms, Mannheim and Heidelberg.

The Westphalia treaty also gave Holland its independence and ushered in the Dutch Golden Age. Amsterdam became the world's biggest port and market for overseas trade. Merchants, scientists, artists and craftsmen thrived in the Renaissance atmosphere, painter Rembrandt (1606–69) being the greatest example. The Dutch East Indies Company expanded into a powerful commercial monopoly establishing trading posts throughout the Far East, in Africa, Brazil and the Caribbean.

French Revolution

The Rhineland enjoyed a rare century of peace until the outbreak of the French Revolution. Exemplary for many German princes in the Age of Enlightenment, the Palatinate's Prince-Elector Karl Theodor founded in Mannheim a music school, national theatre and science academy and promoted porcelain manufacture in Frankenthal. Bonn was an important musical outpost of the influential Mannheim school, and the court organist there had as his prize pupil Ludwig van Beethoven (1770–1827). Johann Wolfgang von Goethe was born in Frankfurt in 1749 and his university days in Strasbourg were momentous in awakening his sense of German identity.

Strasbourg warmly welcomed the French Revolution, which strengthened the city's attachment to France and accelerated the adoption of customs and language. In 1792, Rouget de Lisle, an officer stationed in Strasbourg, composed *La Marseillaise* as a War hymn for the Rhine Army. It was adopted by a regiment of Marseille volunteers and became the rousing national anthem that still stirs the hearts of the French today.

The French Revolutionary army marched into the Rhineland in 1792 and "liberated" Speyer, Worms, Mainz and Frankfurt. Encouraged by the French general Lazare Hoche, German nationalist Joseph Görres campaigned for an independent Rhenish republic, but the project died with Hoche in 1797.

19th Century

The German Rhineland was incorporated into Napoleon's empire in 1806 as the Confederation of the Rhine. Industry and agriculture were developed, new roads built along the river, new schools opened on the model of the French *lycée*, and Jews were emancipated. Initial enthusiasm faded after 63,000 Rhenish troops were conscripted—and almost all killed—in Napoleon's disastrous 1812 campaign in Russia. The Prussians pursued Napoleon back across the ice-covered Rhine at Kaub in 1813. The Congress of Vienna—orchestrated in 1815 by Koblenz-born Austrian Chancellor Clemens von Metternich—ended the French annexation but handed the Rhineland over to Prussia. From 1816 to 1866, Frankfurt was the seat of the German Bundestag. The Prussian monarchy used the completion of

Cologne cathedral in 1842 as a symbol of national unity.

The Prussians suppressed Joseph Görres' too radical newspaper, the *Rheinische Merkur*, but permitted—for six months—the young Karl Marx (1818–83) to edit the liberal *Rheinische Zeitung*. Düsseldorf poet Heinrich Heine fled Prussian censorship in 1831 to go into permanent exile in Paris. Marx wrote his *Communist Manifesto* in 1848, the same year that short-lived revolts swept across Germany, including Heidelberg, Mannheim and Mainz. In Cologne, radicals simultaneously sang the *Marseillaise* and campaigned against French claims to the Rhineland.

German industry expanded in the 1850s, and canals built between the Rhine and the Ruhr made Duisburg Europe's most important inland port. Philosopher Friedrich Nietzsche was appointed to the chair of classical philology at Basle University in 1869, but he was forced to leave ten years later because of a nervous breakdown.

During the Franco-Prussian War (1870–71), Strasbourg was bombarded and annexed to Germany with Alsace-Lorraine. The post-war creation of a unified German Reich produced an industrial boom in the Rhineland and Ruhr region, of which Düsseldorf became the region's administrative centre. Carl Benz built Germany's first motor-driven vehicle in Mannheim in 1885.

Modern Times

At the end of World War I, Cologne was among the industrial cities that revolted in 1918 to form the short-lived Soviet-style workers' and soldiers' councils. But at the Versailles Peace Conference, France's Marshal Foch pushed for an independent Rhenish Republic under French supervision. Rhenish separatists, among them the Mayor of Cologne Konrad Adenauer (the future West German Chancellor), staged a coup d'état on June 1, 1919. They declared a republic with its capital in Wiesbaden, but it lasted only a few hours before Clemenceau, under Anglo-American pressure, sent orders to break it up.

From 1923 to 1925 French and Belgian troops occupied the Ruhr to enforce payment of punitive war reparations. At the beginning of the 1930s, embittered Ruhr industrialists and bankers gave Hitler their financial backing. In 1936, in breach of the Versailles Treaty, Hitler sent the German army back into the Rhineland and celebrated the unopposed reoccupation with an exultant speech in Cologne Cathedral. In September 1938, Britain's Neville Chamberlain came to Bad Godesberg (now a Bonn suburb), praising the "relationship of confidence" he had created with Hitler over Czechoslovakia—two months before the Munich conference clearing the way for the German invasion. In November, 1938, synagogues were burning all over the Rhineland—in Cologne, Koblenz, Mainz and Worms—as part of the nation-wide anti-Jewish Kristallnacht (Crystal Night).

In May 1942 British bombs devastated Cologne in the first of a series of Allied air raids that combined with Hitler's own scorched-earth policy of 1945 to destroy Mainz, Koblenz, Bonn, Düsseldorf, Frankfurt and other major cities in the region. In March 1945 Remagen was the first US Army bridgehead across the Rhine. Unscathed, Heidelberg became the US Army headquarters in Germany in 1952.

In 1946 a new state (Land) united North Rhineland and Westphalia, with Düsseldorf as its capital. Bonn became the capital of the Federal Republic of

(West) Germany in 1949 under Chancellor Konrad Adenauer.

During the 1990s the Ruhr economy switched progressively from coal and steel to cleaner service industries. The equestrian statue of Kaiser Wilhelm I for Koblenz's Deutsches Eck erected in 1897, destroyed in 1945, was resurrected in 1992. The same year, the Rhine-Main-Danube Canal (begun in 1845 as the Ludwig Canal) completed the Main river link with Danube for a continuous waterway from Black Sea via Rhine to North Sea. Frankfurt was chosen as the seat of the Central Bank for the European Union.

Helmut Kohl, who began his career as Rhineland-Palatinate state premier, became Germany's longest-serving chancellor. His defeat in 1998 meant that Chancellor Gerhard Schroeder led the transfer of the Federal German government and parliament from Bonn to Berlin for the year 2000.

Kaiser Wilhelm keeps watch over the Deutsches Eck in Koblenz.

On the Scene

A Rhine cruise demands that you take it easy. Flowing through four countries at the very centre of western Europe, the river could easily give the most avid visitor a bad case of cultural overdose. Along the way, there are great cities to be visited. Otherwise, just sit back and enjoy the view of the castles and cathedrals. Join in the songs when the band strikes up and toast the grand scenery with a cool glass of Rhine or Mosel wine.

▶ FROM AMSTERDAM TO KOBLENZ
Amsterdam, Along the River, Düsseldorf, Cologne, Bonn and Upriver, Koblenz

Amsterdam

At first glance, the city seems to confirm all the images by which we know it. Amsterdam really is a mesh of elegant canals, quaint bridges and old coffee houses. Trams and bicycles continually whizz through the streets. Tulip fields and windmills are only a stone's throw away, and although Amsterdammers have given up clogs for Nikes these days, you'll find the people remain as welcoming as if their city were the friendly village it sometimes resembles.

Mills were an effective means of draining inland expanses of water.

But the picture is more complex. Because of its tradition of openness and tolerance, Amsterdam is also a cosmopolitan mix of cultures. This began as far back as the 17th century, when Spanish Jews and French Huguenots came here to escape from persecution. Today, new Amsterdammers include refugees from Africa and Asia, people from former Dutch colonies such as Surinam and Indonesia, and those who have flocked here since the 1960s, attracted by Amsterdam's relaxed social attitudes on such things as marijuana. Looking closely at those canals, you'll find that their waters reflect a variety of faces, and a living, changing city.

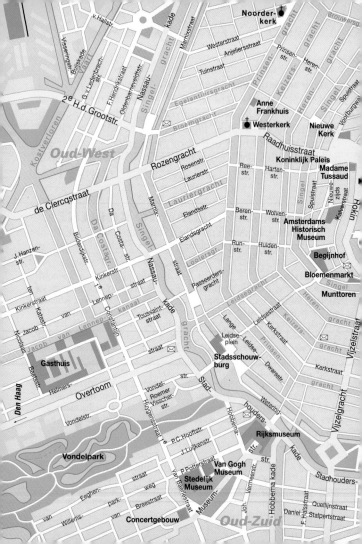

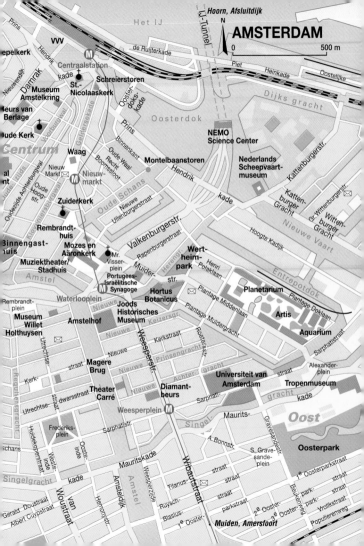

Canal Tour

The one-hour canal tour is the best introduction to the city and shows you Amsterdam in a nutshell—historic and charming, pragmatic and businesslike. Singel, the inner canal, was once the city's fortified boundary. Look out for house No. 7, a real oddity—the narrowest house in Amsterdam—only as wide as its front door and jammed between two 17th-century buildings. Three bridges down, at the junction with Oude Leliestraat, note the iron-barred windows of a quaint old jail set into the bridge itself and just above water level. Approachable only by water, it's said to have been used to keep drunks quiet overnight.

In the early 1600s, the town spread outwards from the Singel to Herengracht, the most prestigious canal during the city's Golden Age. The wealthiest merchants vied with each other to build the widest homes, the most elaborate gables, the most impressive front entrance steps. The patrician houses are still here in all their glory, though most are now too big for private residences and are occupied by banks and offices.

Keizersgracht was named after Holy Roman Emperor Maximilian I, whose realm also included the Netherlands. The houses on this canal are not quite so grand as on Herengracht, but still charming and solid middle-class.

Prinsengracht, the last main canal of the horseshoe, is considerably more down-to-earth, with smaller homes and many warehouses still in their original condition and some transformed into

---

VINCENT VAN GOGH

At the age of 16 Vincent van gogh worked for an art dealer; he abandoned his theological studies in 1883 to turn to painting. His first works depict, in dark and gloomy colours, farmers and labourers of his native Flanders. In 1886 he joined his art dealer brother Theo in Paris. There he became acquainted with the Impressionists, whose influence was soon revealed in his own works, the colours becoming much brighter and his brush strokes bolder. In 1888, Van Gogh moved to Arles, where the Provençal landscape gave him many of his best subjects. He began to show signs of mental disturbance and cut off part of his ear after a quarrel with his friend Gauguin. After a stay in an asylum in Saint-Rémy he returned to Auvers-sur-Oise near Paris, where, a few months later, he had another fit and committed suicide.

luxury apartments. The ubiquitous hoisting-beam for commercial goods is still affixed to the warehouses, but nowadays its main use is in getting the well-off tenants' new sofas upstairs.

Leidseplein

Leidseplein (*plein* means square) is the site of the old city gate on the road to Leiden. Today, the gate, the markets and the carriages have given way to restaurants, outdoor cafés and cinemas, discos, nightclubs and bars.

The northwest side of the square is dominated by the Stadsschouwburg (Municipal Theatre, built in 1894). The American Hotel, virtually next door, is something of a city tradition. A building full of character, begun in 1880, it has a magnificent Jugendstil restaurant, officially protected as an architectural monument. This has become a meeting place for artists, writers and students. Dutch-born Mata Hari, the legendary World War I spy, held her wedding reception at the American in 1894.

Vondel Park

Acting as a "lung" for the densely built city centre, the park was named after Holland's foremost poet, the 17th-century Joost van den Vondel. Its 49 ha (120 acres) include lawns, lakes and flower displays.

Museumplein

This broad grassy square, wild with crocuses and daffodils in spring, is bordered by three major museums and the city's main concert hall. At the top of the square is the palace-like Rijksmuseum, opened in 1885, home of one of the world's great art collections. Besides exhibits of porcelain, Asiatic and Muslim art, 18th-century glassware, and 17th-century dolls' houses, the Rijksmuseum's main attraction is the European art section, and Dutch painting in particular, including Rembrandt's *Night Watch*, which can be seen in the Philips wing while the museum undergoes restoration. The modern Van Gogh Museum houses more than 200 paintings and 400 drawings by Vincent van Gogh. The neighbouring Stedelijk (Municipal) Museum is closed for renovation; meanwhile, part of its collection of international modern art. can be seen in the TPG building near the railway station.

Flower Market

At the top of Leidsestraat along the Singel canal is the 200-year-old floating flower market (*drijvende bloemenmarkt*). A profusion of plants and flowers bedeck the gently swaying shop-boats moored at the canalside. The Munttoren (Mint Tower) overlooks this colourful scene, its 21

It isn't your eyesight—some of Amsterdam's canal houses really do tilt tipsily.

17th-century carillon chiming out an old Dutch tune every half-hour.

Begijnhof

North of the floating flower market, the Beguine Court is hidden behind an arched oak doorway on Spui, opposite a university building. Inside is a neat quadrangle of lawn surrounded by perfect 17th- and 18th-century alms-houses, two small churches and a 15th-century wooden house. The court was originally founded in 1346 for the benefit of the Beguines, members of a Dutch lay sisterhood, replaced today by elderly women citizens.

Historisch Museum

Behind the Beguine Court, the vast Historical Museum tells the city's fascinating story from 1275 to 1945. Exhibits range from prehistoric remains and the city's original charter to audio-visual slide shows on land reclamation.

Dam Square

Bustling Dam Square is the city's hub, dominated by the Koninklijk Paleis (Royal Palace). Opened as the Town Hall in 1655 in the country's Golden Age, it was converted into a palace by Louis Bonaparte, the emperor's brother, during his brief sojourn as king in Amsterdam (1806–10).

Nieuwe Kerk

Just across the narrow Mozes en Aäronstraat stands the New Church. This simple, 15th-century late-Gothic basilica had its slender steeple added in the 19th century. Inside are some splendid baroque woodcarving and 16th- and 17th-century organs.

The white, stone column on the other side of the square is the National Monument erected in 1956 to commemorate the Dutch role in World War II.

Westerkerk

Behind the palace, the West Church was begun in 1619. It boasts Amsterdam's tallest tower, 83 m (273 ft), topped by multi-coloured crown and orb, a replica of the crown presented to the city by Holy Roman Emperor Maximilian I in 1489.

Anne Frankhuis

The house at Prinsengracht 263, is where, from 1942 to 1944, Anne Frank hid from the Nazis, writing her diary. Upstairs at the end of a corridor is the bookcase wall which swings out and gives access to the concealed part of the house. Here Anne, her family and friends survived until betrayed nine months before war's end.

Jordaan

The Jordaan area across the canal has become a fashionable artists' quarter with its inevitable complement of colourful shops, boutiques, restaurants and so-called "brown bars".

Railway Station

The city's main railway station dominating the Damrak boulevard vista is both a considerable engineering feat and a fine 19th-century neo-Gothic monument. It was built on three artificial islands and 8,687 wooden piles by Petrus Cuypers, architect also of the Rijksmuseum.

At the waterfront opposite the station, the NZH (Noord-Zuid Hollands) Koffiehuis houses the tourist office and a restaurant. Just a few yards down Damrak from the station, the former stock exchange building (the Beurs van Berlage, 1903) serves now as a concert hall for the Dutch Philharmonic Orchestra.

Oude Kerk

The Old Church, behind Beursplein, is the city's biggest and oldest (1300). Rembrandt's wife Saskia was buried here. Most of its ornament and statuary was removed by 17th-century Calvinists as "Catholic pomp", but it retains fine Gothic stone carving and stained-glass windows.

Harbour

On the 15th-century Schreierstoren, across the small Chinese 23 quarter of the lower Zeedijk, a plaque proclaims that English-man Henry Hudson left from here to discover Manhattan Island in 1609.

Overlooking the harbour, the Nederlands Scheepvaartmuseum (Maritime Museum) is housed in old Admiralty supply buildings. A replica of an East India Com-pany ship is moored outside.

Nemo

The buzzwords here are interac-tive and hands-on. The technol-ogy museum, located on the Oos-terdok, promises an upbeat, up-to-the-minute encounter with science and technical gadgetry, with a special interest in energy, communications and the amazing world of the human race.

Rembrandthuis

Rembrandt's House at Joden-breestraat 4–6, red-shuttered and three storeys high, is a 1606 brick building with a typical step gable. It was the home of Holland's greatest painter from 1639 to his bankruptcy 20 years later.

Portugees-Israëlitische Synagoge

The synagogue was built in 1675 by the city's large community of Sephardic Jews, descendants of refugees from Spain and Portu-gal. They claimed it followed the plan of King Solomon's temple.

In front of the synagogue, the Dockworker Statue by Mari Andriessen commemorates the courage of Amsterdam's dock-workers who in February 1941 staged a 24-hour strike to protest the deportation of Jews.

Bridges

Just a minute's walk away, River Amstel, from which Amsterdam takes its name, has two splendid bridges: the Blauwbrug, no longer the blue bridge from which it takes its name, but a copy of the gilded Pont Alexandre in Paris, and a picturesque white wooden drawbridge with nine graceful arches, the Magere Brug, or "Skinny Bridge".

Rembrandtsplein

The brash Rembrandt Square and the adjoining Thorbeckeplein are covered with advertising, cinema, restaurant, bar and nightclub signs, offering everything from strip-shows to a cup of coffee at one of the many outdoor cafés.

Amsterdam–Rhine Canal

One of the city's major techno-logical achievements is the Am-sterdam-Rhine Canal, 72 km (45 miles) long and probably the busiest canal in Europe. Connect-ing the port of Amsterdam to the Rhine delta, it handles ocean-going vessels of up to 4,300 tons' displacement.

Along the River

After Amsterdam, the journey upriver from the Dutch hills—yes, Holland does have hills—of Nijmegen across the German border at Emmerich and south to where the Mosel river flows into the Rhine at Koblenz covers a distance of nearly 300 km (almost 200 miles).

Arnhem

For four days in September 1944, Lt Col John Frost and his battalion of 600 British paratroopers held out against overwhelming odds on the bridge over the Lower Rhine. John Frost Bridge, named in his honour, provides the starting point for an explanation of modern Arnhem's appearance. This is where the battle was most ferocious, and from here the city's scars are still visible.

The most prominent victim was the church of St Eusebius, founded in 1452, whose tower was destroyed in the fighting. A new one was built, with no attempt to make it blend into the medieval structure. It dominates the skyline, standing as a symbol of Arnhem's rise from the ashes. A glass lift takes you past the great carillon bells, up to a height of 73 m (240 ft) for a panoramic view of the city, the Rhine and the surrounding countryside. The interior of St Eusebius reflects the typical sobriety of the Dutch Reformed Church, but look out for the marvellous Renaissance marble sarcophagus of Count Karl von Geldern in the choir.

Behind the church is another medieval survivor, the ornate 15th-century Stadhuis. Its nickname of Duivelshuis (House of

---

DOWNSIDE, UPSIDE

Navigable for 870 km (over 540 miles), the Rhine is linked by a system of canals to the Main and Danube rivers that enable big barges (over 5,000 tons deadweight) to sail all the way through from the North Sea to the Black Sea. The rapid increase in the river's cheap freight traffic since the second half of the 19th century has kept the prices of raw materials down and made the Rhine a magnet for large-scale industrial production. Factories along the river are (literally) churning out one-fifth of the world's chemical products. Analysis of the river's water has identified over 6,000 different toxic substances. The positive aspect of this has been that, whereas the Rhine was for centuries the focus of major European wars, these ongoing pollution dangers are forcing the old enemies along the river's banks into peaceful cooperation to find ecological solutions.

the Devil) is derived from the macabre figures carved on its façade.

Most of the streets in this area were laid out after the war. But you can reflect on times past on the Korenmarkt, towards the west of the city. It is one of the oldest squares in Arnhem, and a pleasant place to sit outside on a summer's evening with a drink. This was the centre of the corn trade from the 14th century to the present, but the trading hall in the middle of the square, dating from 1899, is now a cinema.

Outside the centre, the Kröller-Müller Museum houses admirable canvasses by Picasso, Seurat and Mondrian, among others, but the highlight of the museum is a collection of some 278 works by Van Gogh, ranging from his sombre early Dutch masterpiece, *The Potato Eaters,* to later explosions of colour in *Wheatfield with Reaper and Sun* and *Haystacks in Provence.* The sculpture park outside has an extensive selection of sculptures by Barbara Hepworth, Rodin, Moore and Giacometti, as well as monumental surrealistic marvels such as Dubuffet's *Jardin d'Emaille.*

Appropriately, Arnhem has a fine museum dedicated to the events of September 1944. The Hotel Hartenstein at Oosterbeek was General Urquhart's headquarters during the battle and is now the Airborne Museum. Its combination of audio-visual displays, commentaries, photographs and dioramas gives an informative and moving account of the epic struggle that took place in this area. Nearby is the Oosterbeek Military Cemetery, whose rows of headstones speak eloquently of the terrible loss involved. Towards the Rhine, the Old Church of Oosterbeek, built 1000 years ago, was the last stronghold of the British troops trying to escape across the river.

Nijmegen

Just over 100 km (62 miles) east of Rotterdam, Nijmegen has the unique distinction among Dutch towns of being built on hills. Its port stands on the Rhine's main tributary, the Waal, and serves the Maas–Waal Canal on its western outskirts. Since the Romans conquered the Batavian settlement here, naming it Noviomagus, the town has played an important commercial role on the northern waterways. The Carolingian St Nicolaas Kapell, dating back to 799 but modified in the 11th century, is located in the Valkhof park, where Charlemagne and his son Louis built a hunting lodge. On the town's main square, Grote Markt, is a handsome Renaissance municipal weighing-office (Waag) near some fine 17th-century houses.

Emmerich

For southbound travellers, this is the first German town on the Rhine. With the Dutch town of Lobith across the border, it is the Rhine's main customs station. Its redbrick houses with spotless white-framed windows have been neatly restored after World War II bombing, as have the churches of St Aldegundis (1449) and St Martin, of which only the crypt remains from the original 11th-century building.

Rees

A pretty town founded around its medieval convent, Rees has been painstakingly rebuilt after almost total wartime destruction. Across the river, admire the silhouette of Kalkar's parish church and stately 15th-century gabled town hall.

Xanten

It entered history in 15 BC as an important Roman garrison town for two legions guarding the empire's frontiers against Germanic invaders. A 3rd-century Roman amphitheatre has been excavated, and the Romanesque-Gothic church of St Viktor is dedicated to a Roman soldier martyred in the 4th century for his Christian faith. Xanten is identified as the birthplace of Siegfried, hero of the ancient Nibelung saga. The town gate is a splendid twin-towered affair of 1393.

Duisburg

Built at the all-important confluence of the Ruhr river and the Rhine, Duisburg is one of the world's biggest inland ports. The progressive switch in emphasis in the 1990s from steel and coal to electronics and service industries has left the city brighter, greener and with more breathable air. In any case, the town had a guaranteed place on the map, being the home of the 16th-century geographer Gerhard Mercator. The father of modern cartography is buried in the Salvatorkirche; he is honoured with a statue in front of the town hall and his name was given to the new university (1972). The works of another illustrious citizen, expressionist sculptor Wilhelm Lehmbruck (1881–1919), are displayed in the superb museum bearing his name, alongside the 20th-century sculptures of Archipenko, Brancusi, Giacometti and Henry Moore. The shopping streets' fountains are gaily decorated with monumental pieces by Jean Tinguely and Niki de Saint Phalle.

Krefeld

Though the town is resolutely modern, Krefeld's position as a major textile centre for silks and velvet can be traced back to its medieval beginnings in linen-weaving—which continued until King Friedrich II of Prussia granted Krefeld a silk monopoly in the 18th century. This history is traced by the Deutsches Textilmuseum with colourful exhibits of textiles and costumes. Two monuments of early 20th-century domestic architecture, Mies van der Rohe's Lange and Esters houses (1928–30), now serve as museums of contemporary art.

Düsseldorf

Its internationally admired fashion designers, theatre and avant-garde art galleries bring a certain elegance and refinement to the Rhineland. At the confluence of the Rhine and the little Düssel tributary, the town is a key communications centre. It is an important rail junction, active river port with three harbours on the Rhine, and its Lohausen airport is one of the busiest in the country. As the capital of North Rhine-Westphalia (population 580,000), Düsseldorf also serves as banker and book-keeper to the vital industrial belt of the Ruhr district immediately to the north, all the more important since the region switched progressively from coal and steel to electronics and the service sector. Its forward-looking modern image is symbolized by the three eye-catching, crooked towers of the Neuer Zollhof by Californian architect Frank Gehry, looming over the harbour basin.

Königsallee

The city's greatest tourist attraction is its main shopping street. The Königsallee runs straight as an arrow parallel to the Rhine river. Popularly known here as the "Kö", the broad avenue is a delightful piece of urban design with a fountain and waterway running down its middle. Swans glide by in the shade of chestnut trees, as graceful as the fashionable girls swinging their shopping bags along the pavements. Appropriately, the darker, west side of the street is lined with insurance companies and banks, while the east side bathed by the afternoon sun is for strollers. This is the Schokoladenseite, or "chocolate side", where you can sample heavenly German pastries and chocolates on café-terraces or shop in the smart boutiques.

Heinrich Heine monument

After years of neglect, the town has honoured its most talented citizen with the Heinrich Heine monument on Schwanenmarket west of the Kö. This appropriately provocative modern sculpture by Bernd Gerresheim celebrates the great lyrical and mordant ironic poet with a bizarre and grotesque face that seems to be falling apart. It has been suggested that it reflects the writer's merciless dissection of German society in the 19th century.

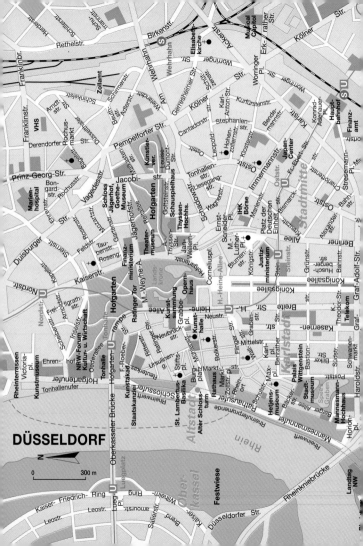

Growing up during the Napoleonic occupation of Düsseldorf, Heine became enamoured of French culture and chose Paris as his place of exile when fleeing what he regarded as the stifling intellectual atmosphere of Prussian rule in 1830.

Marktplatz

In the old town's Marktplatz is an admirable equestrian statue of 18th-century Prince-Elector Johann-Wilhelm ("Jan Wellem"), another fervent Francophile. It is said that he was so popular that the citizens happily donated their silver spoons to be melted down and complete the casting of the statue. Heinrich Heine recalled that, as a little boy, "I stood for hours in front of the statue wondering how many silver spoons were in it and how many apple tarts you could get for all that silver."

St Lambertus Church

Over by the river, the 14th-century stone and brick parish church of St Lambertus is built in characteristic Rhenish Gothic basilica style. The roof of its impressive west tower, 72 m (236 ft) high, was added in 1817. Inside, the elaborately carved 5th-century housing for the sacrament (Sakramentsturm) is a masterpiece of late Gothic sculpture. The baroque high altar and pulpit are 17th-

century. In the deambulatory behind the altar, notice the grand 16th-century wall-tomb of Duke Wilhelm V by Cologne artist Gerhard Scheben.

Hofgarten

Immediately to the north of the Kö is the beautifully landscaped Hofgarten park. Among its many sculptures is Aristide Maillol's *Harmonie*, a gentler monument dedicated to Heinrich Heine. At the northeast corner of the park, the 18th-century Schloss Jägerhof, a restrained baroque hunting lodge, houses a Goethe museum devoted to the manuscripts and letters of the grand master of German literature whom Heine derided for his pompous self-importance and obsequious attitude to authority.

Museums

The great pride of the region's principal art museum, Kunstsammlung Nordrhein-Westfalen on Grabbeplatz is a collection of 88 works by Paul Klee. They are shown with his contemporaries Oskar Kokoschka, Emil Nolde, August Macke and Franz Marc. Dada and Surrealist art is well represented, as are Picasso, Georges Braque and the Americans, Jackson Pollock, Robert Rauschenberg and Franz Kline.

Two other museums are worth a visit: the Kunstmuseum (Mu- 31

The leaning towers of Düsseldorf, designed by Frank Gehry, form an eye-catching harbourfront.

nicipal Art Museum, Ehrenhof 5) for its modern furniture, textiles and industrial design, and above all the splendid Jugendstil glassware in a collection that presents a veritable history of decorative glass from antiquity to the modern era; the Hetjens Museum, Schulstrasse 4, traces with a private collection 8,000 years of German and European ceramics.

Cologne

Capital of the Rhineland, Cologne is one of the oldest and most distinguished cities in western Germany. It lies at the centre of a pious but never austere religious tradition, where good Catholics take a secular, even pagan delight in the joys of the flesh. The great symbol of the Church's abiding authority is Cologne's gigantic, twin-spired cathedral. Yet the town is the scene every year of Germany's most riotous, lusty, frolicking Carnival, when wives put away their wedding rings and the husbands are not at home to complain.

Phoenix-like, Cologne arose after World War II from a rubble-strewn desert to become the proud, businesslike city of today. For now, as in centuries past, Rhinelanders settle down to their romantic dreams only after a hard day's work.

Cathedral

For a taste of the Rhineland's mixture of the practical and the romantic, the serious and the humorous, there's nowhere better to begin than Cologne. And in Cologne the starting point is inevitably the cathedral (Dom).

After the bombardments of World War II, it was one of the few buildings left standing. Today, amid Cologne's shining rebuilt prosperity, elevated on a terrace like a rather haughty dignitary, the cathedral occupies a position that has been sacred since Roman times, when it was the site of the Temple of Mercurius Augustus.

The first Christian church was built here in the 4th century by Bishop Maternus. Gradually expanded, it began to burst at its seams in the 13th century, when thousands of pilgrims flocked to Cologne to view the shrine containing the relics of the Three Kings. In 1248 the church was replaced with a cathedral conceived on a gigantic Gothic plan. Work went on for 300 years and then halted for lack of funds, the steeples still unbuilt. It remained that way for another 300 years until, at the urging of the young German Romantics and nationalists, work was resumed and the steeples finished in 1880. They complete the largest façade—61 m wide, 157 m high (200 by 515 ft)—of any church in Christendom. Inside, the true architectural glory of the cathedral is its choir, a magnificent example of 13th-century Gothic intensity, its slim, almost delicate lines forming a striking contrast to the massiveness of the edifice. Very impressive in their natural elegance, set on the pillars of the choir, are the statues of Christ and Mary flanked by the apostles, sculpted by Master Arnold, one of the building's original architects.

The cathedral's richest treasure, looking itself like a basilica, is the gold Dreikönigenschrein (Shrine of the Three Kings) behind the high altar. The bones of the Three Kings were brought by Friedrich Barbarossa's chancellor, Reinald von Dassel, from Milan in the 12th century. Nikolaus von Verdun was commissioned to design this masterpiece of the goldsmith's art. Begun in 1181, it took 40 years to complete. The solid gold figures include the kings and prophets of the Old Testament along with scenes of Christ's Baptism and the Adoration of the Kings.

Another highly prized work is Stephan Lochner's splendid 15th-century *Dombild*, a triptych to the right of the choir, celebrating the patron saints of Cologne—Ursula, Gereon and the Three Kings.

On the left side of the choir, the fine 10th-century Gerokreuz (Ge- 33 ro Cross), was named after Archbishop Gero who commissioned this movingly simple Crucifixion. In the Sakramentskapelle is the lovely Milan Madonna, sculpted around 1280, with the colour, crown and sceptre restored in the 19th century.

Römisch-Germanisches Museum

Next door to the cathedral is the delightfully pagan Roman tribute to Bacchanalian pleasure, the Dionysos Mosaic. One of the few good things to have happened in Cologne during World War II was the discovery of this marvellously well-preserved work in the course of digging an air-raid shelter. The museum in which it is now housed was built around the mosaic's original site, once the floor of a prosperous 3rd-century Roman wheat merchant's dining room. Dionysos is the Greek name of the fun-loving god the Romans called Bacchus. You can see him leaning tipsily on an obliging satyr while around him other satyrs and nymphs cavort and make music.

Museums

The postwar reconstruction of Cologne has generally been a boon for the reorganization of its museums. Between the cathedral and the river, the modern cultural complex at Bischofsgartenstrasse 1 houses two great art museums and the Agfa Foto-Historama. The Museum Ludwig is devoted to 20th-century art—Picasso, Dali, Klee, Kandinsky and Max Ernst—but it is perhaps most remarkable for the comprehensive American pop art collection. The Wallraf-Richartz-Museum is a triumph of imaginative lighting, and displays an excellent collection of early Rhenish art and many fine examples of the great European painters—Lochner, Dürer and Cranach to name but a few.

The Schnütgen-Museum on Cäcilienstrasse displays some of the best Romanesque and Gothic art produced in the city.

Old Town

For just a hint of what the old town of Cologne used to look like, go back to the river, to the tiny Altstadt between the Gross St Martin church and the Deutzer bridge. Around the old Fischmarkt, along the Salzgasse and across the Eisenmarkt (Ironware Market), you can find miracles of survival and restoration in houses dating back to the 13th and 14th centuries. Now a thriving, neighbourhood of restaurants, antique shops, art galleries and apartments with attractive gardens, the lively atmosphere helps you imagine what it was like in the good old days.

The stained-glass window of the Pentecost was given to Cologne Cathedral by King Ludwig I of Bavaria in 1842.

Hohe Strasse

Cologne also has a bouncing, bustling present attested by the gleaming, pedestrians-only commercial area along Hohe Strasse southwest of the cathedral. Reflecting its taste for things French, the town offers plenty of outdoor cafés. Some of the most agreeable are around Am Hof, where you can linger while contemplating the delightfully kitschy dwarfs and inquisitive tailoress of the Heinzelmännchenbrunnen (Dwarfs' Well), sculpted in 1899.

Churches

You might like to look in on the Antoniterkirche, the main church of the small Protestant community on Schildergasse, and admire Ernst Barlach's 1927 sculpture *Der Trauernde Engel* (Mourning Angel)—to which he has given the features of his fellow artist Käthe Kollwitz (who has her own museum at Neumarkt 18–24).

The best of the city's Romanesque churches, indeed one of the most delicate in the Rhineland, is the St Aposteln west of the Neumarkt on Mittelstrasse. The apse is decorated with blind arcades and graceful galleries. But perhaps the most moving of Cologne's ecclesiastical edifices is the Madonna in den Trümmern (Madonna in the Ruins), the mod-

36

ern chapel built out of the rubble of the old Gothic St Kolumba church on Brückenstrasse. World War II bombardments left standing only the stump of a tower and part of one outer wall. Amazingly, a statue of the Virgin Mary emerged unscathed. Hence the name of the chapel, which Gottfried Böhm designed in the 1950s, integrating modern simplicity with the Gothic remains.

Jewish Quarter

On the western side of the Alter Markt is the proud old Rathaus or Town Hall. Its elegant Renaissance pillared loggia is as warm and inviting as the administrative extension of its modern Spanischer Bau is cold and forbidding. From the Rathaus, the Judengasse, once the main street of the medieval Jewish quarter, takes you to the Gürzenich, home of historic merriment. Cologne's most important secular Gothic building was designed as a dance hall for the city government and its honoured guests. The original building of 1441 was damaged by fire in World War II. Rebuilt, it is still the most prestigious venue for Carnival balls, banquets and concerts, the perfect Gothic complement to the cathedral.

Imhoff-Stollwerck-Museum

To end your visit to Cologne on a sweet note, visit this appealing museum in a riverside setting below the cathedral. It tells the story of chocolate, from pod to praline.

Bonn and Upriver

The city has only reluctantly relinquished to Berlin its prerogatives as Germany's capital, but the 50-year experience has given a new pride to what was once just a sleepy university town. The university is in part housed in the 18th-century archbishop's palace and Hofgarten, now a public park. The town's cheerful rococo atmosphere is most evident on the marketplace around the town hall. From here follow Remigiusstrasse to the Münster. The exterior is a transition between Romanesque and Gothic, heavily restored in the 19th century; the interior is baroque. South of the church, the lovely cloister is an oasis of peace.

Museums

With a museum of the composer's memorabilia, the ivy-covered Beethoven House reminds us that the musical giant was born here in 1770. The Rheinisches Landesmuseum is renowned for two prize prehistoric exhibits: the Neanderthal man's cranium and the bones of a Cro-Magnon couple found just outside Bonn.

The "Museum Mile" (Museum-Meile) along Friedrich-Ebert Allee offers the Kunst-

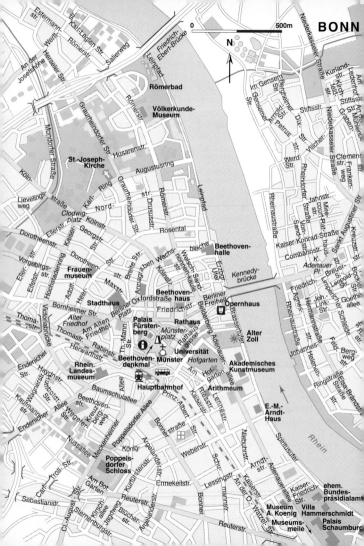

museum, with its permanent collection of German Expressionists such as Bonn's native August Macke, but also Surrealist Max Ernst and avant-garde works by Georg Basleitz and Joseph Beuys; the Haus der Geschichte, with a survey of German history since 1945; the Kunst- und Ausstellungshalle, with major temporary modern art exhibitions; and zoological displays in the Alexander Koenig Museum. Down by the river are the Bundeshaus parliamentary building and the deputies' nearby office skyscraper, nicknamed *langer Eugen* (Long Eugen), after Eugen Gerstenmaier, popular Swabian speaker of the Parliament (Bundestag) in the 1960s.

Königswinter

The village offers a delightful riverfront promenade on foot or in a horse-drawn carriage past charming cafés, restaurants and wine cellars—nothing to do with winter, the name means King's Vineyards. Above it, as English poet Lord Byron put it, "the castle crag of Drachenfels frowns o'er the wide and winding Rhine." It is topped by the romantic ruins of its medieval castle, Schloss Drachenburg.

The peak is part of the Siebengebirge (Seven Hills) from which basalt was quarried to build Cologne and Limburg cathedrals.

Remagen

It is best known for its bridge, which the German army had ordered destroyed before advancing American troops reached it in March 1945. The explosives failed to go off, the Americans got across—and the bridge later collapsed of its own accord. High on a hill above the town, the neo-Gothic 19th-century church of St Apollinaris attracts pilgrims for the saint's festival at the end of July. Opposite, the picturesque little hamlet of Erpel nestles against the formidable Erpeler Ley ("cliff" as in *Loreley* or *-lei*).

Linz am Rhein

In Linz, see the handsome Romanesque parish church, Gothic town hall with its 14th-century carillon and brightly coloured gabled houses of the 17th and 18th centuries. In the hills behind the town are two castles, the 14th-century Burg Ockenfels converted to a hotel in modern times, and the 13th-century Burg Dattenberg, now a romantic ruin. Further upstream, vineyards flank the 13th-century Schloss Arenfels overlooks the spa town of Bad Hönningen.

Bad Breisig

This is a spa resort offering three hot springs and popular for its pretty riverside promenade, its 13th-century church in the upper

town and 18th-century baroque church in the lower town. Looming behind the spa, Burg Rheineck is a largely 19th-century reconstruction that has preserved its medieval castle-keep.

Andernach

One of Germany's oldest towns, Andernach was originally a Roman garrison. It ancient foundations support the sturdy medieval ramparts—look out for the Runder Turm (Round Tower, in part octagonal) on the north side of town. The Romanesque Maria Himmelfahrt parish church dominates the skyline.

Koblenz

Koblenz derives its name from the Latin *confluentes* and has benefited historically from its strategic position at the confluence of the Mosel and Rhine. Besides serving as a centre for the wines of the two valleys, Koblenz used to levy tolls on merchant boats passing from one river to the other. More than four-fifths of the town was destroyed in World War II, but it still offers an attractive glimpse of its past and is a good place to get your first taste of the local wines on offer.

Deutsches Eck

The junction of the two rivers is marked by a monument 37 m (121 ft) high, the huge Deutsches

Eck—"German Corner". Erected to honour Kaiser Wilhelm I in 1897, the original bronze equestrian statue was knocked off its pedestal by artillery fire in World War II. During the 45 years of divided Germany, the great pedestal was preserved as a booster for German unity, reinforced by the monument's original motto: "Never will the Reich be destroyed if you are unified and loyal" *(Nimmer wird das Reich zerstöret, wenn Ihr einig seid und treu)*. Today a replica of the statue, 14 m (45 ft) tall, is back in place and you can climb the 107 steps of the pedestal for a good view of the old town along the Mosel and the more modern construction along the Rhine.

The monument stands at the north end of a pleasant tree-lined promenade along the river bank, the Rheinanlagen. Brainchild of a French prefect during the Napoleonic occupation of the Rhineland, the park was laid out in its present form by Augusta, wife of the Kaiser on horseback. Thirsty strollers stop at the popular taverns of the Weindorf (wine village), a relic of the 1925 wine-fair and still staging popular dances and wine-tasting. North of the Pfaffendorfer Bridge, pass the Kurfürstliches Schloss (Elector-Prince's Palace), an imposing neoclassical structure deprived of its opulent interior by the bombs of 1944.

Beyond the palace, the quay continues to the Romanesque church of St Kastor. Its interior has two Gothic monumental tombs of Trier archbishops Kuno

---

CHANCELLOR METTERNICH (1773–1859)

The Metternichs were time-honoured members of the Koblenz Catholic aristocracy. Klemens was the son of a minister of the elector-prince of Trier. Studying law in Strasbourg from 1788 to 1790 while revolution was raging through France, the ever-prudent and realistic Metternich decided to make for the remoter safety of Vienna. For a Catholic Rhinelander with Germany not yet unified, the Habsburg capital was also a better bet for a diplomatic career than Protestant Prussian Berlin. His realism paid off in arranging Napoleon's marriage to Austrian archduchess Marie-Louise and then, at the Congress of Vienna, keeping a defeated France strong enough to resist Prussia and Russia. His skills in international diplomacy won him the titles of Austrian prince, Sicilian duke and Spanish grandee—as well as lucrative land-holdings in Bohemia, Moravia, Swabia and up and down the Rhine and Mosel valleys.

41

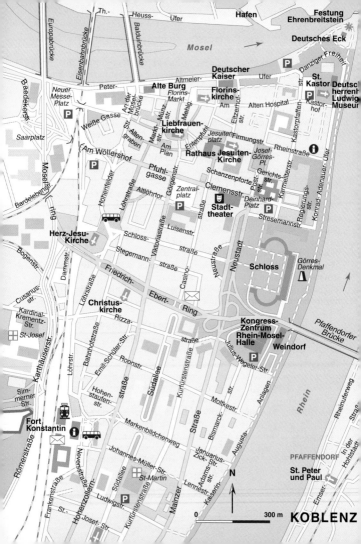

KOBLENZ

von Falkenstein and Werner von Königstein. Open-air operas and concerts are performed in the striking setting of the Blumenhof, courtyard of the Deutschherren-haus (House of the Teutonic Knights), north of the church.

Old Town

Begin your tour of the Altstadt at the Balduinbrücke, the bridge built across the Mosel in 1343 by Archbishop Balduin, brother of Emperor Heinrich VII. It withstood all war and revolution until 1945 when a bomb knocked out three of the 14 arches. Near the bridge, a castle lodge (now housing the municipal library) is all that survives of the old castle (Alte Burg), victim of Louis XIV's French troops in 1689.

On Münzplatz is the Metternich-Hof, the birthplace of the chancellor of Austria, Klemens von Metternich. In the absence of a unified German nation, it was more natural for his old Catholic Rhineland family to turn to Vienna for a diplomatic career, rather than to Protestant Prussian Berlin. Napoleon turned Metternich's house into a law school for the application of the Napoleonic Code to the Rhineland. Münzplatz now has a lively flower, fruit and vegetable market.

Hunt down the few old houses that miraculously survived the war. The oldest, from the 14th century, is at Kastorstrasse 2. The charming 17th-century Vier Türme ("Four Towers"), on the corner of Am Plan and Löhrstrasse, has four projecting oriel bays, a feature of the 18th-century guild halls, that of the grocers on Kornpfortstrasse, that of the cobblers on Görgenstrasse. In war-battered Koblenz they stand out like precious jewels.

Ehrenbreitstein Castle

The medieval stronghold opposite Deutsches Eck was in the year 1000 the redoubt of a knight named Heribert. The archbishops of Trier claimed it for the German empire, the French blew it up in 1801, the Prussians rebuilt it and the Versailles Treaty of 1918 forbade it to be used for military purposes. Today it is a youth hostel, restaurant and museum of prehistoric artefacts, and offers a superb panoramic view of the Mosel and Rhine valleys.

Burg Stolzenfels

The fortress was rebuilt during the nationalist fervour of the 19th century as the quintessential romantic medieval castle, with fanciful turrets and battlements, arches and outer staircases, following plans of the great architect Karl Friedrich Schinkel. It looks across to Lahnstein and its heavily renovated castle, Burg Lahneck at the mouth of the Lahn river. 43

Turning away from the Luxembourg border west of Trier, the German part of the relatively narrow Mosel river flows through a pleasant valley to Koblenz, where it joins the great Rhine. This covers 242 km (150 miles) of the river's total length—545 km (340 miles), from its source in the Vosges mountains in northeastern France.

The meandering Mosel valley's cheerful vineyards and gentle woodland make the cruise a carefree lean-back-and-enjoy-it jaunt. Mosel wine has set the tone for the whole valley—fragrant, pleasant, easy on the palate, celebrated with a festival, wine-tasting or museum in almost every village you stop off at on the way. Names like Piesport, Berkastel-Kues and Cochem bring tears of joy to a connoisseur's eyes. The wine owes its famous bouquet to the fact that the vineyards' often steep slopes capture a maximum of sun in what is Europe's northernmost wine-growing region. But teetotallers, too, like the lusty local cuisine and succulent fruit and fresh juices from the local orchards.

Eltz Castle has been in the same family for 33 generations.

Along the River

The noble remains of feudal castles along the river emphasize the continuing strategic importance of the Mosel in the Middle Ages, both for robber barons and the often rapacious archbishops of Trier.

Winningen

Immediately west of Koblenz, Winningen is surrounded by extensive terraced vineyards and boasts the oldest wine festival in Germany. From late August to early September the town's fountain spouts wine rather than water. Picnickers head up Hexenhügel (Witches Hill) where 21 local women were burned alive as witches during the Thirty Years' War.

Alken

A prosperous trade centre in the Middle Ages, Alken retains several old houses and remains of its medieval fortifications. Behind it towers Thurandt castle, built in 1200 but frequently renovated. In a nearby valley is the enchanting castle ruin of Ehrenburg, dating from the 12th to 16th century.

Burg Eltz

This splendid cluster of edifices put together from the 12th to the 45

16th centuries is surrounded on its hillside by a dense forest. There is endless fantasy in the gables, pepperpot towers and pyramidal roofs, sandstone and half-timbered walls, with look-outs placed here and there. This inspired hodgepodge—still in the family—is the result of dividing up the Eltz inheritance among four sons, each of whom added on his own individual wing. In the 13th century, Archbishop Balduin of Trier felt threatened by the Eltz pile and built his own castle to watch over it from a neighbouring hill, the Trutz-Eltz—"Counter-Eltz".

Treis

With a noteworthy late-Gothic church, Treis is twinned with Karden across the river, an older town founded by the Archbishop of Trier. Its Romanesque church of St Kastor has several fine paintings and frescoes and a 13th-century baptismal font.

Cochem

Undoubtedly one of the Mosel's most picturesque towns is a very popular wine-tasting centre. Centre of activity is the market square with its baroque town hall and flower-bedecked half timbered houses. Visitors can take the

---

MOSEL WINES

It is principally the Riesling vine that gives the wines of the Mosel Valley their unique bouquet. The grape itself is small, delicate, requiring a lot of sun and perfect soil conditions. The valley provides both. At its best, the Mosel bouquet is delicate and subtle, connoisseurs noting fragrances of lime, acacia, orange-blossom, even a hint of cinnamon. It is in general a dry white wine that can be happily drunk not only with all manner of fish and seafood, but also meats, especially the Mosel's locally hunted game.

The finest vineyards are in the central region from Trittenheim to Traben-Trarbach. Its most celebrated wine-centres, where the steeply sloping vineyards have the best exposure to the sun, are at Piesport, Bernkastel, Graach and Zeltingen.

Mosel wines are bottled in green glass, to distinguish them from the brown-bottled Rhine wines. On the label, notice the different indicators to taste and quality. *Kabinett* means light and dry. The late-harvested *Spätlese* will be more gentle and full-bodied. Specially selected *Auslese* produces a richer flavour; *Trockenbeerenauslese*, from grapes in their ultimate state of maturity, gives an almost liqueur-like quality to the wine.

chair-lift up the Pinnerkreuz hill to the edge of the Märchenwald (Fairytale Forest) for a view of the sleepy little town.

Rising beyond the houses on another hill, surrounded by vineyards, is the medieval Reichsburg castle, elaborately restored in the 19th century. Down by the river, but at a safe distance from the yachting harbour, spectacular fireworks displays in summer "celebrate" the burning down of the whole town by the French in 1689.

Beilstein

Beilstein has some handsome half-timbered houses of the 16th century. The family of Koblenz-born Austrian Chancellor Metternich were the last owners of the castle ruins (Burgruine Metternich) here, left by the French forces of 1689 with scarcely more than the pentagonal belfry and an arched doorway.

Marienburg

The convent (12th-century) over on the river's left bank lies now in graceful ruin after closing in the 16th century because the archbishop of Trier disapproved of the nuns' unseemly behaviour. It was destroyed in the Thirty Years' War in successive occupations by the Bavarians, Swedes and French. The French Revolutionary army came back in 1792 to finish it off. The convent commands a lovely view of the valley and rolling vineyards.

Zell

Nestling in a loop of the river, Zell is still protected by the remains of medieval fortifications from the region's tempestuous past. The 16th-century Renaissance palace of the Elector-Prince of Trier (Kurfürstlicher Schloss) has been transformed into an elegant hotel. The parish church, rebuilt in the 18th century, has retained from the originally Gothic edifice a fine wooden statue of the Madonna by a sculptor from Cologne.

NIKOLAUS CUSANUS (1401–64)

The scholarly son of a Mosel fisherman made his mark on the Renaissance world both as philosopher and statesman. His papal masters made him a cardinal for his diplomacy and ideas for monastic reform. They appreciated less his work in mathematics and astronomy. Adopting the name of his birthplace in Kues, Nikolaus Cusanus did not wait for Christopher Columbus to conclude that the earth was round and, long before Copernicus and Galileo, that it revolved on its axis around the sun.

From the old fortifications, you get a great view of Zell and its vineyards.

Traben-Trarbach

This is a double town linked by a bridge. On the Mosel's north bank, Traben is best known for what is left of its Schloss Grevenburg, blown up in 1697. Trarbach on the south bank has some attractive 18th-century half-timbered and late 19th-century *Jugendstil (Art nouveau)* houses and an impressive gateway on the bridge.

Bernkastel-Kues

Another pair of villages standing respectively on the right and left banks of the river and joined by a bridge. With the castle ruin of Burg Landshut looming in the background, the community's wine-growers tend Germany's largest continuous expanse of vineyards, extending north to Graach and Zeltingen. Most celebrated of its vintages is the Bernkasteler Doktor, whose bracing if not medicinal qualities are vouched for worldwide.

There are some splendid half-timbered houses on Römerstrasse, but if some of the taverns seem almost too cute, head for the wine cellars for more serious tasting. The Markt on the Bernkastel side of the river is the popular focus of town life. Notice the old pillory with its iron chain still standing in the northwest cor- 49 ner. The fine Renaissance Rathaus (town hall) overlooks an octagonal fountain (1606) graced by the town's patron saint Michael. The most bizarre of the half-timbered houses, just off the market place, is the top-heavy Spitzhaus (Pointed House) built in 1583, a triumph of will-power over structural stability.

Across the river in Kues is the birthplace of Renaissance humanist scholar Nikolaus Cusanus—Haus zum Krebs—together with the hospital he founded in the 15th century. His heart is buried in the Gothic chapel. Astronomical instruments and other memorabilia of his life are on view in the library.

The Mosel Weinmuseum at Cusanusstrasse 2 offers colourful exhibits on the history of the region's wine makers, their techniques, instruments, glasses and bottles throughout the ages—and a room for wine-tasting.

Piesport

Originally a Celtic settlement known to the Romans as *Porta Pigentio*, Piesport has won an international reputation for what connoisseurs agree to be one of the finest of German wines, Piesporter Goldtröpfchen—literally "Piesport's golden droplets". Before or after your wine-tasting, meditate on life's other high achievements of the spirit in the

opulent rococo interior of the Pfarrkirche (parish church) decorated in 1776 by Trier painter Johannes Peter Weber. Ceiling paintings depict *Mary's Assumption*, the *Fall of the Angels* and Jesuit missionary Francis Xavier preaching to the Indians.

Trier

Trier sits comfortably in the Mosel valley plain, proud of its ancient Roman origins, and has something unmistakeably sunny and Mediterranean about it. In fact, not content with being Germany's oldest city, Trier proudly proclaims it is even older than Rome. A house on the market place bears the inscription *Ante Romam Treveris stetit annis mille trecentis* ("Trier was standing 1,300 years before Rome"). You can still observe the town's Roman origins with a basic urban ground plan unchanged for more than 2,000 years.

Porta Nigra

Access to the town centre continues through the massive Porta Nigra (Black Gate), more fortress than gate. Standing at the north end of town, it faces the road to the Rhine as a formidable bastion against the Germanic hordes. Dating from the 2nd century AD, its sandstone blocks were joined not by mortar but by iron clamps. "Porta Nigra" is a post-Roman

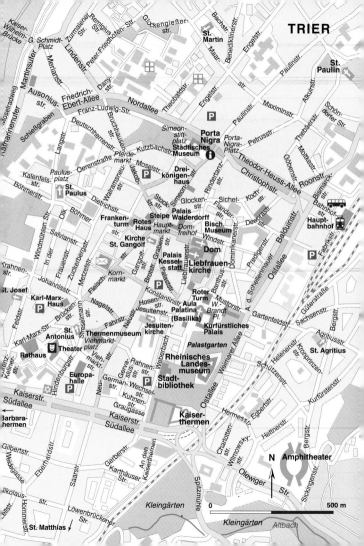

Handsome houses line Trier's market square, around the Petrusbrunnen.

reference to the pollution of the ages, but at the base you can see that the gate was once pale pink.

An archbishop of Trier transformed part of the structure into a Romanesque church, the Simeonsstift. It honours the Syrian monk Simeon who in 1028 came to Trier on a pilgrimage from Jerusalem and shut himself up to die in a cell inside the Porta Nigra. The superb, two-storeyed cloister now houses the municipal museum (and tourist information centre). The ground-floor archways are a beautiful combination of white limestone and red sandstone. The museum has an important collection of church sculp-

ture and monastic furniture from the Mosel region and a new section of modern art.

Dreikönigenhaus

South on Simeonstrasse, notice on the left (No. 19) the rather garishly renovated but still graceful 13th-century House of the Three Kings. In the old days the front door was on the second storey, reached by a staircase that could be removed in case of danger.

Hauptmarkt

The market square is in every sense the heart of Trier, a lively centre for cheerful vendors around the Petrusbrunnen (St Peter's

52

Fountain, 1595) that proclaims the cardinal virtues of Wisdom, Justice, Moderation and Strength. These are the qualities that speak from the stones of Renaissance and baroque houses surrounding the square, lovingly reconstructed from their wartime damage.

South of the square rises the sturdy tower of the 15th-century St Gangolf church, entered through a fine white baroque archway between the house.

Cathedral

Trier's cathedral is massive and fortress-like, a powerful Romanesque structure that epitomizes the town's ancient function as a citadel of the Roman Empire, both pagan and holy. The basic limestone structure dates from the 11th century, but the reddish sandstone masonry goes back to Roman times, the 4th century, and is the earliest-known church building in Germany. Inside, on the south side, notice the pulpit (1572) and Allerheiligenaltar (All Saints' Altar, 1614), both the work of sculptor Hans Ruprecht Hoffman.

The adjoining 13th-century Liebfrauenkirche, pioneer among German Gothic churches, is built on a central Greek cross plan. The interior, with its floor forming a 12-petalled rose, the mystic flower symbol of the Virgin Mary, has an appealing dignity.

St Paulinus Church

Northeast of the Porta Nigra, the St Paulinus-Kirche is one of the

---

KARL MARX (1818–83)

The great philosopher of socialist revolution was the grandson of a rabbi, but his lawyer father converted from Judaism to Lutheran Protestantism when Karl was six years old. He left Trier to study law in Bonn and Berlin and took a philosophy degree in Jena. His radical ideas on liberal economic theory as editor of the Cologne-based *Rheinische Zeitung* caused the newspaper to close in 1843. Exiled to Paris, he developed his socialist ideas in a lifelong partnership with Friedrich Engels, producing the *Communist Manifesto* in the revolutionary year of 1848. His final home was in London, where he spent most of his time in the British Museum Library. He made a name for himself as a bitter and brilliant polemicist, correspondent for the *New York Tribune*, predecessor of today's *International Herald Tribune*. He is buried in London's Highgate Cemetery but his ideological heart remained in Germany where, he was always convinced, the Communist revolution would ultimately triumph.

region's most important baroque churches. The slender, elegant edifice was designed in the 1730s by the Bohemian-born architect Balthasar Neumann, with ceiling paintings by Thomas Scheffler.

Rheinisches Landesmuseum

The regional museum, at Ostallee 44, offers a fine insight into the Rhinelanders' life under the Romans. Among the wall-paintings, mosaics and sculptures, the outstanding exhibit is the stone carving of a Roman wine ship (AD 200), loaded up with barrels and a grinning sailor who looks as if he has been sampling the merchandise.

Spielzeugmuseum

Popular with children and adults alike is the Toy Museum at Nagelstrasse 4. Its reserves of 5,000 pieces make it the largest private collection in Germany, including dolls, mechanical toys and superb model trains.

Kaiserthermen

The Imperial Baths date from the early 4th century AD. At the eastern end is the wonderfully preserved caldarium hot bath-house. To the west was a domed tepidarium and a frigidarium with five swimming pools, next to a dressing room, massage parlour and steam bath. At the other end of the Kaiserstrasse, turn left on

Friedrich-Wilhelm-Strasse to the cosier Barbarathermen, 200 years older than the Imperial Baths. The ruin is nicely overgrown with moss, grass, ivy and wild flowers. At the Mosel, see the Römerbrücke (Roman Bridge) with its 18th-century arches on 2nd-century pillars.

Karl-Marx-Haus

From the bridge, Karl-Marx-Strasse takes you directly to Brückenstrasse 10, birthplace of this Catholic town's most famous and most un-Catholic son. Surrounded by sex shops and strip-joints, the Karl-Marx-Haus has a fascinating collection of memorabilia of the founding father of the Communist movement. Besides private and public letters, his most famous text, *Das Kapital*, is here in manuscript form, along with photos of the young Marx with all the great revolutionaries of his day.

Luxembourg

Some river cruises offer excursions into the Grand Duchy of Luxembourg, with the opportunity to explore the grand old capital and continue afterwards to the French city of Metz.

The small, landlocked country of green hills, forests and castles doesn't owe anything to fairytales. Its encounters with the armies tramping from east to west and back again are real enough, and more numerous than those of any other European nation.

The capital, Luxembourg City, was built in a spectacular location, on a high rocky bluff rising steeply from the gorges carved out by the rivers Alzette and Pétrusse. From Roman times onwards, when it stood at the junction of the great Paris to Trier and Metz to Aix-la-Chapelle roads, its strategic significance was never lost on Europe's military leaders. This impregnable situation made it a plum to be picked in turn by the Romans, Huns, Franks, Burgundians, French, Germans, Spanish and Austrians. But nowadays, with a population of 80,000, the capital resembles any other successful commercial European city, with sprawling suburbs, glass and concrete highrises and more than 250 banks. However, if you approach from the east, and see the lofty bastion sheltering behind its massive fortifications, you can almost imagine you have been transported back in time.

Despite hundreds of years of foreign occupation—or perhaps because of it, Luxembourgers have a keen sense of national identity, expressed in their language, Lëtzebuergesch, a local dialect of German. In fact they are trilingual, also speaking French and German.

Luxembourg City

Sigefroi built his fort on a promontory called the Rocher du Bock; all that survives today is the base of a circular tower and a belfry on one side and traces of a tower on the other. The city walls were reinforced and extended twice by local rulers. A century after Sigefroi, 15 forts were added, including the Porte de Trois Tours (Three Towers Gate) and outer ramparts. Construction in the 14th century included three new forts carved out of the rock face. Under Louis XIV, the great French military engineer Vauban built the monumental Citadel du St-Esprit, on the site of the Convent of the Holy Spirit, to keep close watch over the lands to the south.

The most remarkable part of the fortifications, the casemates, comprise a 21-km (13-mile) network of underground passages hewn from the rock to link 53 forts. Begun by the Spanish in 1674 and expanded by the Austrians in the following century, these echoing chambers housed not only men and horses, but also armouries and workshops, abattoirs, bakehouses and kitchens. The visit starts at the "archaeological crypt" on the Montée de Clausen, with an audio-visual show creating special sound-and-light effects, narrating the history of the site.

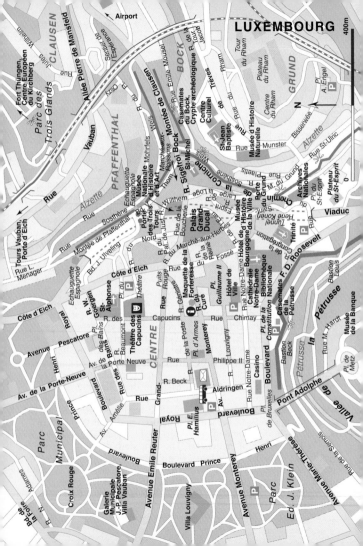

The Chemin de la Corniche is a promenade following the 17th-century ramparts around the edge of the Old City. It leads through numerous gates, some dating back to the 10th century, and barracks with walls 36 m (120 ft) high in places. Little flower-filled parks are set around it so you can sit on a bench and admire the view over the gorges to the bustling modern districts set on the plateaux all around. To the north you can see the Charlotte Bridge soaring 280 m (920 ft) above the Alzette, leading to the gleaming buildings of the European Centre where the Court of Justice and various other EU parliamentary offices are grouped around Place de l'Europe.

The old town grew up behind the Bock, focusing on the point where the Roman roads crossed at the end of Rue Sigefroi, just past the 17th-century St Michael's Church. This area is now called the Marché aux Poissons (Fish Market), where many historic buildings still stand. A group of well-preserved town houses, in Gothic, Renaissance and baroque styles, have been renovated to house the fascinating National Museum of History and Art. You can spend hours exploring its collections which span every era from prehistoric and Gallo-Roman times through the Middle Ages, the 16th to 19th centuries to contemporary painting and photography. The museum also holds temporary exhibitions and organizes children's workshops.

For an atmospheric approach to the city residence of the Grand Ducal family, cross over from Marché aux Poissons into the narrow, winding Rue de la Loge. Many of its buildings have retained medieval features above the doors and windows. Or you can take the more direct route via rue de la Boucherie. The imposing Palace of the Grand Dukes occupies the main wing of the former town hall, which was built in the 16th century, 20 years after the first town hall was blown up by a gunpowder explosion. An extension called the City Scales was added in the 18th century, and the Chamber of Deputies annexed in 1859. Guided tours of the Ducal Palace are organized from mid July to end August; enquire at the Tourist Office.

The palace fronts the Rue du Marché aux Herbes. Follow it down to where it meets Rue du St-Esprit and you will see the glass-fronted Museum of the History of the City of Luxembourg: six floors of exhibits recounting the city's architectural, social and cultural past.

Now you can explore the delightful shopping streets of the old town. The tree-lined Place 57 d'Armes at its centre is an ideal place to people-watch while you linger over a drink or a meal at one of its many pavement cafés. Open-air concerts are performed here, and there's always plenty of activity, day and night.

The Tourist Information Office, in the City Hall, is the place to pick up maps and brochures, and enquire about guided tours, excursions, special exhibitions and cultural events. Behind it in the Cercle Municipal is a miniature replica of the fortress built by the French army at the beginning of the 19th century, with a 15-minute sound-and-light show describing the history of what they like to call the "Gibraltar of the North".

Wine villages

Many of the cooperative wine cellars are open to the public; organized tours will show you winegrowers' villages such as Schwebsange, Wellenstein and Remich, and take you for a boat trip on the river. If you overdo the wine-tasting, stop off at Mondorf-les-Bains, a pleasant spa whose mineral waters are said to do wonders for the liver and various other digestive disorders.

The principal wine-growing town in this region is Grevenmacher, linked to Germany on the other side of the Mosel by a bridge.

Metz

After centuries of invasion from the east, the French Moselle *département*'s capital can at last sit back and enjoy the distinctive pleasures of a river dividing into several arms as it flows through the city. The town was founded 3,000 years ago by the Gallic tribe of Mediomatrici from which it derives its name.

On the River Moselle's south bank, the fine Gothic Cathédrale Saint-Etienne was built from the 12th to the 16th centuries. With its lofty nave, the church's windows present a veritable history of stained-glass from medieval portrayals of *St Paul's Life* to Chagall's 20th-century accounts of *Jacob's Dream* and *Abraham's Sacrifice* in the apse.

In a convent on Rue du Haut-Poirier, the Musée de la Cour d'Or traces the town's history from Gallo-Roman times. Outstanding are the 7th-century chancel screen's carved wooden panels from the Early Christian church of St-Pierre-aux-Nonnains. Its European paintings include work by Delacroix, Corot, Vuillard and Picasso.

The Old Town is grouped mainly around the arcaded Place St-Louis with its characteristic stone-buttressed houses from the 14th to 16th century. The Porte des Allemands is an imposing bastion left over from the old city

Luscious tarte aux mirabelles, made from the sun-blessed local produce.

walls. The rest were removed by the town's most recent invaders in 1870, the Prussians. Berlin architect Jürgen Kröger gave the town its modern shape, most notably in his startling neo-Romanesque cathedral-like railway station.

River Saar

The landscapes of the Saar between Mettlach and Saarburg are no less romantic than those of the Mosel. The town of Mettlach nestles in one of the prettiest parts of the region, called the Saar-schleife (Saar Bend). There are several interesting buildings, such as the 10th-century Alte Turm (old tower) and the baroque Benedictine convent, where the famous porcelain manufacturers Villeroy & Boch set up a factory in the 19th century. A museum relates their history.

Downriver, Saarburg is a beautiful medieval town. Its houses huddle together along the river banks, guarded by the fortress that gave the town its name. The towers of the parish church of St Lawrence stand out on the skyline, though they seem quite small compared with the huge nave. Another interesting feature of the town is the bell foundry (Glockengiesserei), in activity since 1770 and open for visits. 59

Rhine Valley

The stretch at the legendary heart of the Rhine Valley, between Koblenz and Mainz, is just 93 km (58 miles) long. Since the invasion of Julius Caesar's Roman armies, much history has been packed into the region, from the Middle Ages and Renaissance when Mainz was ecclesiastical capital of Germany and home of Gutenberg's printing press, to the modern era when Napoleon incorporated the region into his empire as a French département. The spa town of Wiesbaden provided a major base for the US armed forces after World War II.

Braubach

With its charming riverfront rose gardens, half-timbered houses and medieval turreted city-walls, Braubach is best known for its magnificent Marksburg castle. Erected around 1100 and expanded until the 17th century, it was the only fortress in this part of the Rhine Valley to escape unscathed from the 1689 invasion of Louis XIV's armies. Its armoury room, torture chamber, kitchens, ladies' apartments have all been

Katz, the toll-collector's castle, is now a private school.

preserved, as well as the medieval botanical garden and outer stairway for cavalry carved in the rockface.

Boppard

This is a cheerful town surrounded by vineyards. The tree-lined Rheinallee promenade passes the Alte Burg and beautifully restored medieval buildings like the house of Ritter (Knight) Schwalbach. Remains of the massive Roman ramparts are in places 9 m (29 ft) high. On the market place, over the site of the Roman baths, is the twin-towered Gothic church of St Severus, the town's patron saint. Inside are two fine sculptures of the Virgin Mary and the crucified Jesus, both from the 13th century. The Karmeliterkirche has an admirable Renaissance interior, in particular its choir stalls.

A chair-lift on the northern outskirts takes you up to an observation point known as the Four Lakes View (Vierseenblick) where, because of a bend in the river and other natural obstacles, what you see are not four lakes but four stretches of the river.

Kamp-Bornhofen

The town attracts pilgrims to a "miraculous" *Pietà* in its 13th-

century Gothic church and convent. You can visit an interesting museum devoted to the Rhine boatmen (Flösser- und Schiffermuseum). Above the town loom two restored medieval castles referred to as *"die feindlichen Brüder"* (Enemy Brothers): Burg Sterrenberg and Burg Liebenstein.

Burg Katz and Burg Maus

The little Mouse Castle, officially Thurnberg, looks down its hill at the bigger Burg Katz on the right bank just north of St Goarshausen. Burg Katz (Cat Castle) was built at the end of the 14th century by Count Johann von Katzenelnbogen (whose name means "cat's elbow") to gain control of the river tolls that were previously collected by Maus.

St Goarshausen

The town is little more than a long row of houses, many of them from the 16th century, hugging the river bank beneath terraces of vineyards. On the town hall, a stone plaque proclaims the date of its façade, 1532, in Gothic, Greek and Hebrew characters. On the opposite bank, St Goar is dominated by a picturesque castle ruin, Burg Rheinfels, built by a Katzenelnbogen ancestor in 1245 and reduced to a romantic heap by French troops in 1797.

Lorelei

The siren who inspired Heinrich Heine's melancholic poem sat on the rugged tree-covered cliff bearing her name on a bend in the river south of St Goarshausen. At its best in the evening sunshine described by the poet, the ledge offers a grand view across to Oberwesel and Schönburg castle and down the crag from which the lady lured sailors to their doom in the Rhine's swiftly flowing waters.

Oberwesel

Its remarkable city walls count no less than 18 towers around the perimeter. In its red sandstone Gothic Liebrfrauenkirche is an impressive altar dedicated to St Nicholas. The Schönburg castle ruin now has a hotel within its precincts.

Kaub

This is the spot where General Blücher led his Prussian troops across the ice-covered river on New Year's Day, 1814, to pursue Napoleon's army back into France. North of the town is Burg Gutenfels, restored in the 19th century and now a hotel. Out in mid-river, the 14th-century castle of Pfalzgrafenstein, was originally a massively fortified toll-booth.

Bacharach

According to a 13th-century German scholar, Bacharach derived its name from the Latin *Bacchi ara*, a Roman altar of Bacchus. In

---

FATAL ATTRACTION

With or without a karaoke microphone, everybody joins in the Lorelei song, at least the first four lines:

> *Ich weiss nicht, was soll es bedeuten,*
> *Dass ich so traurig bin;*
> *Ein Märchen aus uralten Zeiten,*
> *Das kommt mir nicht aus dem Sinn.*

Düsseldorf-born Heinrich Heine was 26 when he wrote his poem of the Lorelei legend. Jilted in turn by his cousin Amalia and her sister Therese, he was in a state of despondency. The *Lorelei* was one of dozens of poems into which he poured his misery, half-suicidal, half-ironic. The beautiful siren with the golden hair, golden comb and golden necklace was undoubtedly his cruel, beloved Therese. And the poor woeful sailor in his little boat, bewitched by her song and dashed to death on the rocks below, was of course Heine himself.

Noise and merriment fills Rüdesheim's tavern-lined street, Drosselgasse.

fact, the town is not that ancient, but visitors to this enchanting wine village usually find the old sage's etymology to be convincing. The lovely half-timbered Altes Haus (1568) and other flower-bedecked homes, especially attractive around the marketplace, confer a peaceful atmosphere. Not that the community was always so innocent, as attested by a ruined chapel, the Wernerkapelle, on a slope above the town. It commemorates the death, in 1287, of a boy named Werner. At the time, superstitious bigotry claimed he was ritually murdered by the Jews, which justified their massacre and con-

fiscation of their property. A French army, landslides and an earthquake have turned the chapel into a romantic shell overgrown with wild flowers and shrubbery.

The medieval Burg Stahleck was restored in the 1920s and is now youth hostel with a grand view of the river.

Lorch

The Gothic church of St Martin is notable for its 15th-century high altar, carved choir stalls and a Crucifixion of the 13th century. Wine-lovers visit the stately Hilchenhaus, a splendid aristocratic mansion dating back to the

1540s and now used for tasting the local vintages.

Assmannshausen

The town proposes one of the Rhineland's few good red wines. It has been produced here at least since the 12th century and was a favourite of that great bon vivant, Otto von Bismarck. People also come here today for the warm bromide of lithium waters at the Kurhaus to cure their rheumatism or lumbago.

Bingen

One of the Rhine's main communication centres—river port and railway junction—Bingen was badly battered in World War II. But it's a good place to taste the excellent local wines. The most picturesque of the reconstructed churches is the Rochuskapelle. Out in the middle of the river is the garish yellow tower of the old customs-post. Despite spoilsport scholars who dispute the name, the Mäuseturm (Mouse Tower) is forever associated in popular imagination with a gruesome legend surrounding the end of a prince of the church, Archbishop Hatto of Mainz.

Rüdesheim

This is perhaps the best-known of the Rhineland's wine villages. Its Drosselgasse is crammed with the liveliest collection of taverns

and wine-cellars in the region. Here, in an atmosphere of perpetual festivity, try the Rheingau's famous Rieslings, sparkling Sekt and locally distilled brandies. Find out how it is all done in the Rheingauer wine museum at the Brömserburg castle. Most of the original timber-framed houses were bombed in World War II, but the reconstructed replicas are weathering nicely. In the Obergasse, the Brömserhof has kept its Gothic and Renaissance buildings intact.

A cable-car takes you up above the Rüdesheim vineyards to the Niederwald-Denkmal, or Ger-

NO MORE MR MICE GUY

During a periodic famine, Archbishop Hatto of Mainz (850–913) showed no mercy for the people, who were begging for food. He locked up the ringleaders in a barn and set fire to it. "Listen to the squeals of my little mice," he said as he walked back to his palace. The fire killed the starving trouble-makers but also drove out thousands of mice from the hay and into the archbishop's palace. Horrible Hatto fled to the Bingen tower in the middle of the river, but the little mice followed and ate him up.

mania monument, a 10.5-m (35-ft) statue of an extremely Teutonic lady brandishing the imperial crown. This extravagant exercise in 19th-century nationalism inspires awe in some, in others wry amusement at best. The monument was erected in 1883 to celebrate the unification of Germany following the defeat of France in the war of 1870–71. The best reason for the ride is the wonderful view of the valley.

Wiesbaden

The capital of Hesse enjoys the mellowest climate of all the Taunus spas. This elegant resort is noted for its fashionable boutiques along Wilhelmstrasse.

The Städtisches Museum (municipal museum) has some good German art—Lucas Cranach, Bartel Bruyn, Max Beckmann, Lovis Corinth and Max Liebermann—as well as the Russian Alexey Jawlensky.

In the Kurpark, take a snooze among the flowers and shrubs at one of the many open-air concerts or stroll off for half an hour into the pretty Rambach valley.

Mainz

Over the centuries, Mainz has played many roles. It has been a key part of the Roman Empire's northern defences, an indispensable element in the Vatican's control of Catholic Europe, a major trade centre in the Middle Ages, the home of printing pioneer Johannes Gutenberg and a focus of intellectual ferment in Germany's rise to national unity. That all sounds very serious, but Mainz also takes much of the credit for the Rhineland's reputation for cheerfulness. It's madly merry during the Carnival, even managing a grin in the face of countless invasions and wars. And none was more destructive than the last, World War II, which destroyed four of every five buildings. After a slow and painful reconstruction, the town today has retrieved its prosperity, liveliness and good humour.

Cathedral

The cathedral epitomizes the character of the town and its people—plump, ruddy in complexion and, despite its monumental proportions, somehow cosy and intimate. Get an overall view from the old cemetery southwest of the church. Typically for the Rhineland, the Romanesque basilica has chancels at either end, each with a majestic tower: on the east the austerely simple construction of the 12th century and on the west a more ornate synthesis of Romanesque, Gothic and baroque.

Fires, wars and even rapacious building speculators removing the masonry have stripped the

interior of much of its old riches. But reconstruction has been heroic and some splendid works of art have survived.

Enter by the 13th-century Market Porch (Marktportal) with its 1000-year-old bronze doors. Of 45 archbishops buried in the cathedral, 29 have magnificent monumental tombs. The most important, at the west end of the nave, are three 16th-century sculptures by Hans Backhoffen of archbishops Uriel von Gemmingen, Jakob von Liebenstein and Berthold von Henneberg. Note the elegant rococo choir stalls in the west chancel.

The St Magnus chapel left of the east high altar has a superb 15th-century sculpture group of the *Burial of Christ*.

With a cathedral that has suffered as much as this, its museum is worth a visit to see the statuary salvaged over the centuries. Notice in particular fragments of the 13th-century rood screen. One of the statues is of the architect, plainly groaning from an aching back for having to serve as a pillar for a doorway.

Market Square

On the square north of the cathedral is Germany's oldest Renaissance fountain, the splendid Marktbrunnen commemorating Karl V's victory over the French at Pavia and dating from 1526.

Gutenberg Museum

On Liebfrauenplatz, the museum is a modern building incorporating the old 17th-century inn, Zum Römischen Kaiser. Since 1962, it claims the grand title of World Museum of the Art of Printing (Weltmuseum der Druckkunst). It traces the history of men's efforts to communicate by writing, from primitive stone and papyrus via a Gutenberg Bible and movable type to the most modern sophisticated technology. Homage is paid to the Koreans who developed printing techniques before Gutenberg, while the Mainz master's workshop is reconstructed in the basement.

Old Town

Mainz is a major centre for the wine trade, holding a popular wine fair in the Volkspark at the end of the summer. You can sample German wines year round at the Haus des Deutschen Weines on Gutenbergplatz.

But before you do so, get a feel for the old town of Mainz by exploring the triangle leading from the cathedral along Ludwigstrasse and around to the river on the Grosse Bleiche. Among the fine baroque residences are Dalberger Hof on Klarastrasse, now the police headquarters, Bassenheimer Hof on Schillerplatz and the Erthaler Hof, Schillerstrasse 44.

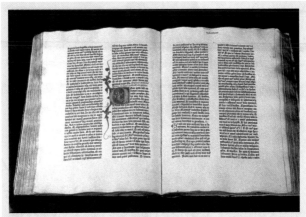

Gutenberg's 42-line Bible: of the original 180 copies printed, 48 have been preserved. Colour was added by hand.

PANDORA'S BOX

A goldsmith by trade, Johann Gutenberg (c.1390s–1468) at first dabbled with printing as a secret sideline. His aim was to reproduce the design of medieval religious manuscripts by a process of move-able type. Wooden printing blocks were too slow and unwieldy, so he worked on a new metal alloy and an oil-based ink that could, for the first time, print on both sides of the paper. He developed most of his techniques during a politically motivated exile in Strasbourg in the 1430s, but returned to Mainz to set up his first press in 1446. His most famous production is the Gutenberg Bible—also known as the 42-Line Bible for the number of lines in each column. Debts forced him to hand over his invention to his business partner, fellow goldsmith Johann Fust, but he was able to bounce back with the sup-port of Mainz's Prince-Elector, Archbishop Adolf von Nassau. The Catholic Church may have regretted this patronage half a century later when Gutenberg's hardware enabled Protestants to spread right across Europe the software of Martin Luther's incendiary tracts.

The Main river flowing into the Rhine at Mainz is often referred to as Germany's "equator", dividing the country's north and south. Many claim that the valley marks a change in character—cooler, more disciplined to the north, more relaxed to the south. Gastronomes have even noted a corresponding change in cuisine: the south's taste for pork, sausages, dumplings and Spätzle noodles giving way at the Main to the north's preference for beef, mutton, more fish and green vegetables. Passing through the regions of Hesse and Franconia, travellers can happily get the best of both worlds—washed down by some excellent Rhine wines at the Mainz end of the trip and the light Franconian wines as they approach Würzburg.

Frankfurt

At the heart of Germany, Frankfurt has been at the crossroads of continental trade since the Bronze Age. Even when the city's political fortunes were waning, there were other fortunes to be made—

The world meets up at Frankfurt's trade fair grounds, at the foot of the pencil-shaped Messeturm.

from passing traffic and annual trade fairs. To this day the fairs attract visitors year-round; particularly well attended is the Book Fair, held each October in the Messegelände.

Frankfurt has long outgrown its early boundaries; the ancient city was originally guarded by ramparts arching in a semicircle to the north of the Main, but no more than a small segment of the 12th-century wall still stands. Sachsenhausen, a settlement on the south bank, has come within the city's limits, as have the more far-flung suburbs of Höchst, Bergen-Enkheim and Seckbach, to make up a prosperous conurbation of 3 million inhabitants, 630,000 in Frankfurt itself.

Old Town

Some of the original buildings of the Altstadt have been reconstructed since World War II. Close to the Mainkai, the Römerberg is a pleasant square with many historical associations. The fountain in the middle, with its graceful statue of Justitia (1543), was spared by the bombing, but it no longer gushes with wine as it did for imperial coronations. The Römer, one-time city hall, dominates the square. Its distinctive 71 gabled façade comprises three buildings—from left to right, Alt Limpurg (1495), Römer (1405) and Löwenstein. Inside, the magnificent Imperial Hall (Kaisersaal) provided a worthy setting for the imperial coronation banquets held here from 1562. The portraits present a complete pack of 52 Holy Roman Emperors from Charlemagne to Franz II.

Across the square, Nikolaikirche (St Nicholas's Church) was once the chapel of the city hall, although it pre-dates the Römer by three centuries.

Behind the Römer, the Historisches Museum incorporates the Saalhofkapelle, the oldest surviving building (1175) in the town centre and all that remains of the once-great palace of the Emperor Friedrich Barbarossa.

Cathedral

The cathedral (Dom) dates from the 13th to 15th centuries, but archaeological evidence points to the existence of a Carolingian church from 852 beneath its foundations. More a parish church than a bishop's seat, the cathedral has had its moments of glory; here, between 1562 and 1792, the German emperors were crowned. The austere interior has some finely carved 14th-century choir stalls. To the right of the choir is the simple Election Chapel (Wahlkapelle), where the elector-princes (Kurfürsten) met in conclave. Inside the tower hall, see the splendid sculpture group of the Crucifixion by Mainz artist Hans Backhoffen. The Gothic sandstone tower, with 383 steps, offers a commanding view of the countryside; unfortunately it is not usually open to the public.

Goethehaus

Goethe, Germany's most illustrious poet, was born in Frankfurt in 1749. His family house on Grosser Hirschgraben has been restored and furnished authentically; the adjoining building is now the Goethemuseum.

New Town

Beyond the bounds of the Altstadt, Frankfurt's alter ego takes over. The Neustadt dates from the 17th century, but it continues to be the hub of commercial activities. The focal point is the square, An der Hauptwache, watched over by a baroque guardhouse, the Hauptwache, built in 1730. Goethe was baptised and confirmed in the Protestant Katharinenkirche across the square.

Financial District

Dwarfed by high-rise structures of glass and steel, the Eschenheimer Turm presides over the financial district. Standing 47 m (154 ft) high, this round, five-spired gate to the ancient city symbolizes

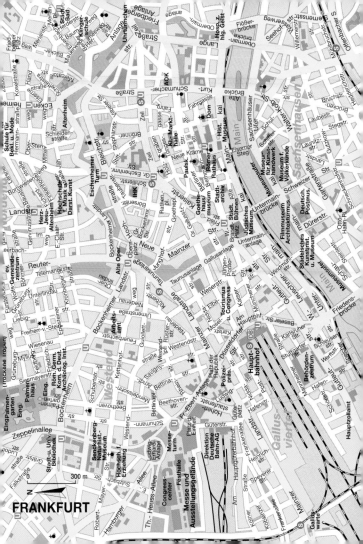

FRANKFURT

Johann Wolfgang von Goethe—lost in reflection?

Frankfurt's former glory as an influential and privileged free state. The 1950s Post Office Communications Centre does at least acknowledge its antecedents: features of the 18th-century palace of the Prince of Thurn and Taxis, one-time Minister of the Imperial Post, have been incorporated into the façade. The Börse, an Italianate Renaissance building of 1879, is now Germany's largest stock exchange.

Messeturm

At the trade fair grounds *(Messe-und Ausstellungsgelände)* is the huge Messeturm, designed by Chicago architect Helmut Jahn.

The red granite 60-storey tower is 256 m (839 ft) high, with offices for the Deutsche Bundesbank at the top and an elegant restaurant at the bottom.

Sachsenhausen

This suburb on the south bank of the Main escaped lightly from both destruction and reconstruction. The old district captures a little more of the atmosphere of bygone times: it was once a village presided over by the powerful order of Teutonic Knights who arrived here in 1221. Their surviving house, the Deutschordenshaus (1705), contains a fine collection of Roman artefacts.

Historisches Museum

In characteristic businesslike manner, most of the museums are grouped on the left bank of the river along Schaumainkai. But many first-time visitors like to start out near the Römerberg at the Historisches Museum, Saalgasse 19, to get a feel for life in days of yore. A scale model of the city shows what the war destroyed. Exhibits from the 15th century to the modern day include an artisan's kitchen and the imperial banquet table, set for the coronation feast. In front of the cathedral, a Historical Garden reinforces the lesson with excavations of the town's Roman settlement and foundations of a Carolingian royal palace.

Museumsufer

Amid the pleasant greenery of Museumsufer (literally "river bank of museums"), a group of neoclassical patrician houses provides a handsome setting for the city's great art collections.

The most prestigious museum is the Städelsches Kunstinstitut, Schaumainkai 63. Created in 1816 from the collection of Johann Friedrich Städel, a banker, the art works are more personal than stately or monumental. At the entrance to the galleries of European art (14th century to the present) is Tischbein's famous portrait of Goethe in a classical Italian landscape (Goethe in der römischen Campagna). Italian masters include Fra Angelico, Botticelli and Pontormo; Dutch and Flemish: Vermeer, Rembrandt and Van Eyck; German: Holbein, Grünewald and Dürer. From the 19th and 20th centuries, the French: Courbet, Monet, Matisse and Degas; German Expressionists Dix, Beckmann and Kirchner.

The German Architecture Museum, Schaumainkai 43, displays with models and master drawings the whole world of architecture from the Italian Renaissance of Bramante and Michelangelo to the most recent innovations of Tokyo, Paris or Chicago.

The Film Museum, Schaumainkai 41, is enjoyable any day but particularly when it rains. The cinémathèque shows three or four classics daily, often accompanied by a 1926 Wurlitzer organ. Cinephiles can trace technical developments from the 17th-century magic lantern and 19th-century peep-shows to the Lumière brothers' cinematograph.

New York architect Richard Meier's design for the Applied Arts Museum (Museum für Kunsthandwerk), Schaumainkai 17, incorporates the neoclassical Villa Metzler into a gleaming modern structure of white enamel and glass. There are superb collections of Persian and Chinese ceramics, Meissen, Sèvres and Nymphenburg porcelain, Venetian and modern American crystal and Art Deco book binding.

The Ethnology Museum (Museum für Völkerkunde), Schaumainkai 29, illustrates the cultures of Africa, Asia, Oceania, North and South America. It contains a beautiful collection of tools, weapons, costumes and exquisite masks and sculpture, with particular emphasis on Bolivia, Ethiopia, Sumatra and Java.

Back on the river's right bank at Untermainkai 14, the new Jewish Museum (Jüdisches Museum) is housed in the restored neoclassical Rothschild-Palais (1821), home of the banking family which sent its sons all over Europe to create a great financial empire. The museum traces the history of Jewish Frankfurt, reproducing parts of the old ghetto, and Jewish roles in German life in general.

Along the River

The Main, 524-km (327-miles) long, rises from two sources—the Red Main and White Main—in the north Bavarian Fichtelgebirge mountains near Bayreuth. Navigable west of Bamberg, it has long been an important east–west trade route, even more so since the new Ludwig Canal linked it to the Danube, creating a continuous waterway from the Black Sea via the Main and Rhine to the North Sea. The Main has no less than 40 hydroelectric plants, the biggest at Griesheim.

Beyond Frankfurt, the Main's eastbound cruise turns south on its picturesque route from the parks and Renaissance palace of Aschaffenburg. This is the heart of the beautiful Spessart hills with their forests of oak and beech trees. After a side-trip east to Mespelbrunn's fancifully restored romantic castle, the river flows on past the flowery, half-timbered façades of Miltenberg and the medieval ramparts of Gemünden and Karlstadt. Journey's end is Würzburg, with the baroque opulence of its bishop's palace and monumental Gothic sculptures of Tilman Riemenschneider surrounded by sunny vineyards. From there it's just a short hop to picturesque Rothenburg ob der Tauber.

Aschaffenburg

The town owes its charm to the opulent tastes of the archbishops of Mainz and more recently Bavaria's King Ludwig I. The archbishops' 17th-century Schloss Johannisburg incorporates a medieval castle keep in a gigantic Renaissance palace built four-square around an inner courtyard. The palace art gallery displays works by Hans Baldung Grien and Lucas Cranach.

In the grounds west of the palace is the Pompeianum, Ludwig I's whimsical replica of the house of Castor and Pollux at ancient Pompeii. Cypresses, fig and almond trees bring the Mediterranean to the Main Valley.

Southwest of town, Schönbusch is the prettiest of Aschaffenburg's lovely parks, designed in the "natural" English manner by Friedrich von Sckell.

Mespelbrunn

This fairytale castle lies 20 km (12 miles) southeast of Aschaffenburg. Restored in 1904, its Renaissance towers are mirrored in a pond at the edge of the Odenwald forest. Inside, the most impressive room is the Knights' Hall *(Rittersaal)* with 17th-century weapons and armour from the Thirty Years' War. In the nearby Hessenthal pilgrimage church and chapel are fine sculptures by Mainz master Hans Backoffen and Würzburg's Tilman Riemenschneider, as well as imposing funeral monuments to the Echter family who built Mespelbrunn castle in 1419.

Miltenberg

The narrow sloping market square, popularly known as the

Bucolic surroundings in Schönbusch Park, Aschaffenburg.

KARLSTADT'S ICONOCLAST

The town achieved renown during the Protestant Reformation movement as the birthplace of Andreas Bodenstein (1480–1541). Teacher, friend then foe of Martin Luther, he took the name of Karlstadt. The fiery theologian led a campaign to destroy the statues and paintings in churches, following a strict interpretation of the Old Testament commandment against graven images.

Schnatterloch (Gossip Hole), is one of the country's most attractive town squares. Against a backdrop of beech trees framing Mildenburg castle above the square, tall, steep-roofed russet and white half-timbered houses surround a handsome octagonal red sandstone well. They include the old municipal wine-cellar, which now houses a museum of the town's history and folklore. On Hauptstrasse, the grand Hotel zum Riesen is reputed to be the oldest princely hostelry in Germany—they say that Emperor Friedrich Barbarossa stayed here in 1158. During the Thirty Years' War, its guests included Sweden's Gustav Adolphus and his arch-enemy, German general Wallenstein—but not on the same day.

Wertheim

The town is dominated by a massive castle ruin, formidable fortress dating back to the 12th century. Among the many fine half-timbered houses on and around the old Marktplatz are the impossibly tapering Bäckerei Kachel, the 16th-century Adler and the Witt house with its frieze of skeletons. Its Gothic parish church, built in 1384, has an impressive series of tombs, the most spectacular being the 17th-century decidedly cheerful yellow alabaster monument to Count Ludwig von Löwenstein-Wertheim and his wife Anna.

Gemünden

At the confluence of the Saale and Main rivers, Gemünden was badly damaged in World War II, but on the ring of its medieval city-walls, the Mühltor gate still stands, as do some houses of the 16th and 17th century. Beyond town on a high spur between the two rivers is the ruin of the 13th-century Scherenburg castle inside a triangle of ramparts.

Karlstadt

The walled town has retained its ancient checkerboard street-plan around the four-square marketplace. The town hall is notable for the fine Renaissance furniture of its council chambers. In St Andreas parish church, the carved pulpit is by Tilman Riemen-schneider and his workshop, with another of the master's sculptures, St Nikolaus, in the sacristy.

Würzburg

The illustrious bishopric lies in the heart of Franconia's wine country. Vineyards spread up the slopes around the Marienberg citadel overlooking the town from across the Main river. This Renaissance fortress houses the Mainfränkisches Museum of regional art and folklore, including ancient wine-presses. But the most cherished works are the Gothic sculptures of Tilman Riemenschneider, who made Würzburg his home from 1483 to 1531.

Residenz

In the episcopal princes' Residenz designed by Balthasar Neumann and Lukas von Hildebrandt (1744), the city possesses one of the finest baroque palaces in Germany. Start out with an overall view from the attractive gardens. Inside, Giambattista Tiepolo painted the *Europa* fresco over the grand ceremonial staircase, as well as those in the oval Kaisersaal (Imperial Hall) depicting Würzburg's medieval history. Neumann's triumph is the Hofkirche, the court church flooded with light and colour. Tiepolo contributed an *Assumption* and the *Angels' Fall from Heaven* for two side altars.

Neumünster

Another fine baroque church is the Neumünster, its noble façade attributed to Johann Dientzenhofer. Inside, a Riemenschneider Madonna in stone stands in the south east niche of the rotunda. The church is the burial shrine of St Kilian, the Irish missionary martyred in Würzburg in 689. The neighbouring cathedral (re-

---

TILMAN RIEMENSCHNEIDER (1460–1531)

Far from being marginal bohemians, the artists of the Renaissance era were often respected members of the community. Like the great painter Lucas Cranach over in Wittenberg, sculptor Tilman Riemenschneider also served as mayor of his city. During the Peasants' War of 1525, the conservative-minded artist surprised his citizens by telling them to open the gates of Würzburg and let the rebels in. After the war, Riemenschneider lost his office and fortune but, unlike 62 other rebels, not his head. He conveyed his personal misery in the groups of mourners sculpted in his last years.

79

built since destruction in 1945) is dedicated to the monk. On the south side of the transept, three Riemenschneider sculptures of Jesus, Peter and Andrew have been placed in a modern stone setting.

Rothenburg ob der Tauber

This town south of Würzburg is the quintessence of Germany's most romantic era, an appropriate highpoint on the Romantische Strasse. Medieval ramparts, monumental gates and lofty gabled half-timbered houses, beautifully preserved, recall Rothenburg's past glories. As its name suggests (ob means "above"), Rothenburg ob der Tauber is built on heights

over a river valley. Serving as a natural moat beneath the town's western walls, the Tauber river has its source 14 km (8 miles) south of town and joins the Main river 120 km (75 miles) to the north. The town's wealthy patricians enjoyed special privileges in the German empire and commissioned great works of art for their churches from Tilman Riemenschneider and Friedrich Herlin.

Marktplatz

There is no more central and historic place from which to begin your walk around town than the Tourist Information Office, on the north side of Marktplatz. The 15th-century Ratstrinkstube is the Alderman's Tavern where Georg Nusch got in

Rothenburg, as quaint as can be.

his training for the famous *Meistertrunk*. (The figures on the old clock go into action on the hour from 11 a.m. to 3 p.m. and from 8 to 10 p.m.) The ground-floor offices were once an open gallery for the town's official weights and measures. Notice, too, the square's monumental Georgsbrunnen (George's Fountain, 1608), one of the many wells needed to raise water to the town's difficult elevated position, essential both for drinking and fire-fighting.

Rathaus

The imposing Rathaus is an apt expression of Rothenburg's civic pride during its medieval and Renaissance glory. Facing south, the Gothic building (1250–1400) houses the Imperial Hall (Kaisersaal). Anyone tackling the stairs to the top of the 60-m (196-ft) belfry gets a splendid view over the town and Tauber valley. To the east, the Renaissance façade (1572–78) added a fine arcade in 1681. The handsome doorway leads to a courtyard, scene of the colourful Christmas market.

St Jakobskirche

The Gothic church behind the town hall was built in 1311 as a pilgrimage church for its revered relic of the Holy Blood. For the Heilig-Blut Altar in the upper chapel, Tilman Riemenschneider's poignant *Last Supper* sculpture (1505) is one of the masterpieces of Bavarian art. Earlier works include the splendid late Gothic sculpture and painting for the high altar (1466) by Friedrich Herlin (from nearby Nördlingen) and some fine 15th-century stained-glass windows in the choir.

MEISTERTRUNK: THE DRINK THAT SAVED A TOWN

Staunchly Protestant in the Thirty Years' War, Rothenburg faced total destruction by the invading Catholic army in 1631. To win over its commander, Count Jean Tilly, the city elders plied the inveterate beer-drinker from the Low Countries with strong Franconian wine. Finally, he agreed to dissuade his troops from the usual fire, rape and pillage if any burgher could quaff in one draught a giant tankard of the wine—13 measures totalling 3.5 liters. Ex-mayor Georg Nusch duly performed what became known as *der Meistertrunk*. The epic tipple is commemorated in spring, summer and autumn with a costumed play and is re-enacted several times a day by figures on the clock of the tourist office.

Municipal Museum

Nestling against the northwest city wall, a 700-year-old Dominican convent houses the Reichsstadtmuseum. Its exhibits include the monastic kitchens, medieval and Renaissance furniture, utensils, weapons, interesting memorabilia from the old Jewish community and, yes, Nusch's original tankard.

Ramparts

To the west, the Hohenstaufens' castle has long gone, but the massive Burgtor city gate (1360) still stands, leading to the Burggarten (castle gardens) with a good view of the Tauber valley.

The best point from which to view the ramparts, which have remained intact since the 13th and 14th centuries, is from the old Hospital (Spital) and the Spitalbastei, a bastion guarding the south end of town. For a walk along the ramparts, start out from the tower of the late-Gothic St. Wolfgangskirche, a veritable fortress in itself adjoining the Klingentor gate. The walk continues east to the Galgentor (Gallows Gate) where criminals took their own last walk. If you want to see how they were treated before being hanged, visit the Kriminalmuseum in the old Johanniter monastic buildings (1395). Here you can see 1,000 years of cruel and all too common punish-ment—barrel-cages for drunks, spiked chairs, racks, suspended iron cages for heretics, chopping blocks and worse.

Main-Danube Canal

In 1992 the boldest dreams of Charlemagne and Ludwig I of Bavaria were realised when the Main–Danube Canal between Bamberg and Kelheim was completed, opening to seagoing ships a 3,500-km (2,170-mile) waterway linking the North Sea with the Black Sea.

Work on the canal began in the Middle Ages—a considerable technical achievement, though it remained unfinished. The Ludwigskanal, with 100 locks punctuating its 177-km (110-mile) length, was inaugurated with pomp in 1846, but increasing competition from the railways proved disastrous. Further work was undertaken in 1922, the stretch from Bamberg to Nuremberg became navigable in 1972, and in 1992 the final stretch to Kelheim was inaugurated. The resulting canal is 171 km (106 miles) long, has 16 locks, and at Hilpoltstein reaches 406 m (1,332 ft) above sea level, the highest point on the European waterway network. Its economic importance is incalculable: in 2000 alone, some 8.5 million tonnes of goods were transported between Bamberg and Kelheim.

However, leaving aside all the technical achievements, a trip on the Main and the Danube is first and foremost a chance to experience a unique landscape and an opportunity to make acquaintance with the customs and culture of Franconia and Bavaria.

Ochsenfurt

About 20 km (12.5 miles) upstream from Würzburg you reach Ochsenfurt, whose town walls date back to the 14th century. The old timber-framed houses on Hauptstrasse are particularly pretty with their wrought-iron signs. Here you will also find the late-Gothic Rathaus (town hall), one of the finest in Franconia. Its musical clock has become the emblem of the town.

The Andreaskirche (13th–15th centuries) has a richly decorated interior with a sculpture by Tilman Riemenschneider.

Kitzingen

The former importance of Kitzingen, one of the oldest towns on the Main (8th century), is apparent from its Renaissance town hall and several churches dating from the 15th to 18th centuries. Parts of the town walls still remain.

Volkach

The attractive little wine-growing town of Volkach, on a loop of the Main, is worth a visit for its fine Renaissance town hall (1544) and the Schelfenhaus, a baroque mansion built by a wealthy merchant, Schelf, in 1719. The pilgrim church of St Maria im Weingarten (St Mary-in-the-Vineyard) lies 1 km to the northwest of the town, and boasts the sculptor Riemenschneider's *Rosenkranzmadonna* (Virgin of the Rosary).

Schweinfurt

The biggest industrial centre of Lower Franconia has been destroyed several times over the centuries, most recently in World War II. Nevertheless, some buildings remain to attest to its historic importance as a free imperial city, among them the late-Romanesque Johanniskirche (altered several times), the town hall (16th century), the former Gymnasium (grammar school), now the town museum, and the Zeughaus (armoury).

Hassfurt

This delightful Franconian town lies 28 km (17 miles) further on. Its late-Gothic Ritterkapelle (Knights' Chapel) boasts a heraldic frieze with 241 coats of arms, together with interesting tombs. The Gothic Pfarrkirche (parish church) contains several works of art, including a wooden sculpture of John the Baptist by Tilman Riemenschneider.

83

Bamberg

The episcopal city of Bamberg is where the Main–Danube Canal begins. The old town is graced with works by the sculptor Riemenschneider and the architect family Dientzenhofer. Take a good look at the cathedral, Bamberg's greatest attraction, where the transition from Romanesque to Gothic can be clearly traced. It houses the tomb of Emperor Heinrich II and his wife, a work of Riemenschneider's, as well as the Bamberger Reiter, a remarkable Gothic equestrian statue. On Karolinenplatz stand the late-Gothic Alte Hofhaltung (the former episcopal palace, now housing the historical museum) and the early baroque Neue Hofhaltung (also called the Neue Residenz). The latter, designed by J.L. Dientzenhofer, has on the first floor a gallery of paintings by German masters, and on the second you can admire grand chambers with antique furniture and tapestries. There's a fine view of the old town and the Benedictine abbey of St Michael from the rose garden. On an island in the River Regnitz, which once separated the castle district from the bourgeois quarter, stands the Altes Rathaus (Old Town Hall), decorated with 18th-century frescoes. The picturesque fishing quarter of "Little Venice" (Klein Venedig) lies on the right bank.

At the end of August, the old town is the site of an exuberant fair. Along with hearty Franconian dishes you can enjoy a glass of Bamberg's speciality: smoked beer (Rauchbier)!

Bayreuth

Make a side-trip to Bayreuth, known for its annual festival of Richard Wagner's operas. The composer's home, Villa Wahnfried, is now a museum containing stage sets, costumes and musical memorabilia. Wagner is buried in the garden with his wife Cosima, daughter of Liszt. The the Markgräfliches Opernhaus, by two theatre designers from Bologna in the 18th century, is a charming baroque creation, with three galleries festooned in stucco trimmings.

Nuremberg

A fine-looking town, Nuremberg (Nürnberg) can once more look with pride on its distinguished history. A centre of medieval culture and veritable heart of Renaissance art north of the Alps, it has also always been at the forefront of German industry and commerce. Today, with a population of 500,000, it dominates the northern Bavarian region of Franconia.

In modern times, its reputation as a generous champion of social progress was sullied by the party

rallies held here by Hitler's Nazis. But outside those bitter, catastrophic years, the city is also known as the home of Hans Sachs's *Meistersinger*, of painter Albrecht Dürer, of master craftsmen who invented the pocket watch, the clarinet and splendid mechanical toys, and of the builders of Germany's first stretch of railway—to Fürth 6 km (3.5 miles) away. Today, besides its ever-thriving toy manufacturing industry, Nuremberg turns out many of Europe's best trucks, tractors and motorcycles, but also sewing machines and pencils.

Since the devastating bombs of World War II, the town has been rebuilt, and its historic monuments have taken on their old patina. The renewed tradition of craftsmanship is honoured with a toy fair every February and an inventors' exhibition every September. The grand Kaisersburg castle recalls old imperial glories. Churches and museums have preserved the best of the town's great sculptures and paintings, and pride of place goes to the Gothic house that was Albrecht Dürer's home in the 16th century.

Some old houses have been converted into handsome restaurants, where you can taste Nuremberg's savoury cuisine, not least its famous little sausages, especially tasty with the Franconian white wines.

Berching

The small Bavarian town of Berching greets the visitor with a skyline straight out of the Middle Ages: the town ramparts (constructed around 1450), with 13 towers and four gates, are intact, and you can walk along some sections of the walls.

Riedenburg

The present-day health resort of Riedenburg on the River Altmühl became a market town in the 13th century, protected by three castles. The valley of the Altmühl is popular with nature lovers, hikers, canoeists and cyclists alike.

The Jagdfalkenhof (Falconry Lodge) at Schloss Rosenburg, built in 1112 gives daily demonstrations with large birds of prey.

Kelheim

At Kelheim the Altmühl flows into the Danube; this is the end of the Main–Danube Canal. The remains of the medieval walls and gates of this town, founded around 1200, can still be seen. Note the Gothic parish church and the elegant façades of the baroque town houses.

To the west of Kelheim, the 45-m (147-ft) Befreiungshalle (Liberation Hall), built by Ludwig I of Bavaria to commemorate the wars of liberation fought against Napoleon, crowns the Michelsberg.

After the Napoleonic Wars, Weltenburg monastery lay abandoned for 40 years until Ludwig I of Bavaria came to its rescue.

Weltenburg

The Benedictine monastery stands in a setting full of natural drama, where the Danube breaks a narrow gorge through the hills of the Franconian Alb. This is where the Christianization of Bavaria is supposed to have begun in the 7th century. The monastery was founded by a Bavarian duke, Tassilio III. The monastery church, a late-baroque jewel, was built in 1716–18 by the Asam brothers, who were active in south Germany but also further afield in Bohemia and Silesia. Earthly pleasures are catered for by the beer from the monastery-run brewery.

Regensburg

Like Bamberg, Regensburg survived the war unscathed, revealing itself in full historical splendour. The city hails back to Roman times, when the mighty Porta Praetoria was built: it stands near the cathedral. The diocese was founded in the 8th century, and from this time princes and emperors held their Diets in the city. Regensburg's heyday was the Middle Ages, and to this day the magnificence of the merchants' houses attests to their wealth and prestige. The Steinerne Brücke (Stone Bridge) is the oldest surviving bridge in Germany (12th-century), and con- 87 nects the main part of the city with the settlement on the other bank of the Danube. The beautiful old city is dominated by the magnificent Petersdom cathedral, with its two 105-m (344-ft) towers, the pièce de résistance of Gothic architecture in Bavaria. The cathedral houses many treasures. The church of St Emmeram dates back to the 8th century but has the Asam brothers to thank for its sumptuous baroque interior. The finest secular building in the city is probably the Old Town Hall.

Regensburg is not only a city of music and culture, but also of good Bavarian cooking: the Alte Wurstküche (Old Sausage Kitchen) is believed to be Germany's oldest restaurant!

A short distance downstream, a huge pseudo-Grecian temple towers above the Danube, resplendent in white marble: this is Walhalla, built for Ludwig I of Bavaria. Climb the 358 marble steps from the moorings to the temple, which houses busts of eminent Germans.

Straubing

Straubing lies in the fertile Dungau, the heart of the Bavarian granary. Every August, the town is the scene of a lively two-week festival. In the picturesque Altstadt (Old Town), see the 14th-

Passau lies at the confluence of the Danube, Inn and Ilz.

century Stadtturm with its five spires on Hauptplatz; Theresienplatz and Ludwigsplatz are surrounded by elegant patrician houses. One of the finest churches is the Ursulinenkirche, designed by the Asam brothers. Straubing's oldest place of worship is a short distance out of town: the Peterskirche, built around 1200. One of the churchyard's three chapels is devoted to Agnes Bernauer, a barber's daughter who fell in love with Duke Albrecht III of Bavaria, and was drowned as a witch in the Danube when Albrecht's father got wind of their unsuitable marriage.

Passau

Austria is but a stone's throw away from the "Town of Three Rivers". Passau was already important and wealthy in the Middle Ages, thanks to the trade in wine, grain and salt, and until the 15th century even Vienna was within the sphere of influence of the powerful diocese. Ships moor directly below the proud Veste Oberhaus castle, which today houses a craft and history museum. Gothic and baroque, the Stefansdom towers above Residenzplatz; it boasts the largest church organ in the world.

South of Karlsruhe, the Rhine forms the natural boundary between Germany and French Alsace. Here, Strasbourg appropriately provides the seat of the European Parliament and a Winstub (wine bar) or two for you to compare the Rhine wines with those of Alsace. Basle, in Switzerland, is the Rhine's southernmost port and the terminus for its sea-going vessels. The city straddles the river and looks into all three countries from the heights of its cathedral terrace.

Wine Country

In the vineyards of Nierstein and Oppenheim, you can sample their whites along with the region's famous Liebfraumilch and Palatinate *(Rheinpfalz)* wines produced further south.

Nierstein

Nierstein can claim as its greatest attraction its world-renowned vineyards on the river's left bank. Together with Oppenheim immediately to the south, it reigns supreme among the wines of Rhine-Hesse with the prestigious Niersteiner Domtaler.

Speyer's mighty cathedral was an imperial burial place.

Oppenheim

Its 14th-century Gothic Katharinakirche is noted for the medieval stained-glass windows in the nave and east choir. Albert Schweitzer gave recitals on its organ. You can visit the church's charnel house (Beinhaus). Many wine cellars are open for tastings, and the German Wine Museum is entertaining and informative.

Gernsheim

On the opposite bank, just 20 km (12 miles) upstream at a bend in the river, the old fishing village of Gernsheim served as a port in Roman times and is now the focus of the Maria Einsiedel pilgrimage.

Worms

Worms has a unique place among the three faiths that have marked Germany's history. The great Catholic monument is the Romanesque cathedral which, like that of Mainz, has two apses, each with twin round towers flanking lower octagonal towers over the transept crossings. The massive structure is lightened by dwarf galleries around each of the towers. Inside the main entrance, the Gothic south porch, notice the 12th-century sculpture of Christ enthroned. The grand baroque altar is by Balthasar Neumann.

North of the cathedral, the 19th-century Luther Monument (Lutherdenkmal) marks the Protestants' place in Worms' history, commemorating the Reformation leader's challenge to the Catholic Church at the Diet of Worms in 1521. Luther is surrounded by other church rebels, including England's John Wycliffe, the Czech Jan Hus and Italy's Girolamo Savonarola.

In the 11th century, when Jews made up a third of the population, the city was the home of Raschi, the great Talmudic scholar Rabbi Schlomo ben Itzhak. Next door to the little Raschi-Haus museum in the Hintere Judengasse stands the oldest stone-built synagogue in Europe (1034). Repeatedly destroyed—not by war but by the local citizenry—it was rebuilt in the 1960s with much of the original masonry.

Ludwigshafen

The industrial port is barely 150 years old, built on the site of a small 17th-century fortress. Its chemical factories have recovered from almost total destruction in both World War II and a disastrous chain of explosions in 1948.

Mannheim

On the right bank, at the mouth of the Neckar river, Mannheim has regained its dual role as a cultural centre and thriving industrial port. In the 18th century, the Palatinate princes transferred their residence here from Heidelberg, to a splendid baroque palace. The city soon became one of the great centres of European music and theatre, attracting Mozart and Schiller as resident artists. Its ultra-modern theatre has renewed the tradition. The palace has been restored along with other baroque buildings such as the Jesuit church and Rathaus (town hall). The Städtische Kunsthalle houses one of Germany's finest collections of 19th- and 20th-century art. A side-trip along the pretty green Neckar Valley takes you to Heidelberg, whose castle is perhaps Germany's most romantic ruin (see page 105).

Speyer

The imposing silhouette of its cathedral proclaims the historic importance of this Imperial town. German emperors were buried in the cathedral, and princes met here to debate the Empire's response to the Reformation. Dating from 1060, the cathedral has twin steeples flanking broader domed towers over the apses, east and west. In the Imperial crypt (Kaisergruft) beneath the southern transept lie four emperors and

---

THE RHINE GOLD

The Rhineland is shrouded in many a spectacular legend. One of the most famous, the epic story of the Nibelungs from the region's deepest Dark Age, inspired Richard Wagner's grandiose opera cycle, "The Ring". The Nibelungs are evil dwarfs, keepers of a magic hoard of gold with a curse on it.

Siegfried, a brave prince from the north, wins the treasure away from them and goes on to the royal palace at Worms to woo Kriemhild, sister of King Gunther. For his part, Gunther lusts after the fierce Icelandic queen, Brünhild, and Siegfried offers to go and get her. It takes a lot of brute force and treachery to bring back Brünhild to marry Gunther. When she finds she is not getting Siegfried himself, she has him killed by Gunther's henchman, Hagen.

Poor widowed Kriemhild hopes at least to hold onto the Nibelung treasure, only to see even that snatched away by Hagen and dumped into the Rhine. To get her revenge, she finds just the right fellow, Attila, marries him and gets his Huns to punish Brünhild, Hagen and company in one of their usual bloodbaths. Since then, nobody has bothered to dredge the murky waters of the Rhine to find that treasure.

four kings, three empresses and a princess, and five bishops. Near the main entrance is the 15th-century Domnapf, a giant sandstone wine-bowl. It is traditionally filled with the local wine for the citizenry to toast new bishops.

The Wine Museum claims, among its wine-presses, barrels and pruning tools, Germany's oldest-known wine, a 3rd-century Roman vintage, preserved by the bottle's stone-hard resin sealing.

Karlsruhe

This industrial city was founded in 1715 as the court residence of the Margrave of Baden-Durlach, later the duchy of Baden. As such, the city has been laid out in formal classical pattern, almost like a French garden, a semi-circle of streets fanning out south of the baroque castle, completed by another semi-circle of gardens to the north. It is the seat of Germany's high courts, and a major cultural centre for the southwest. Its Staatliche Kunsthalle has major works by Grünewald, Hans Baldung Grien and Dürer. It is also an important gateway to the Black Forest.

Strasbourg

As the capital of Alsace, situated at the Rhine river frontier between France and Germany, Strasbourg has a many-faceted identity. French since the 17th century, it is the most patriotic of cities, celebrating Bastille Day on July 14 with special fervour. It was here, not in Marseille, that the national anthem, the *Marseillaise*, was composed. Strasbourg's German roots are present, too, in the Alsatian dialect, in the Rhenish architecture of its great cathedral, its gabled, half-timbered houses reflected in the waters of the River Ill, the little tributary of the Rhine, but also in its steaming plates of *choucroute*, as they call *sauerkraut*, and in its fine beers and even finer white wines—Riesling and Gewürztraminer—tasted in the town's Winstuben (wine bars). The many university students that gather there can count among their more illustrious alumni Johann Wolfgang von Goethe and the Austrian chancellor Klemens Metternich.

Cathedral

At the very heart of the city centre is one of Europe's most distinguished monuments, the great cathedral. With its single north tower and steeple rising from one side of the façade, the asymmetrical silhouette has a startling impact on any unsuspecting newcomer. Appropriate to Alsace's Franco-German legacy, this masterpiece of Gothic architecture draws on design elements from cathedrals in the Rhineland and the Ile-de-France, the region around Paris. The splendid pink sandstone façade was begun by master builder Erwin von Steinbach in 1277, but he got only as far as the grand Gallery of Apostles over the central rose window. A century later, Ulrich von Ensingen, architect of Ulm's huge cathedral, added the octagon for the north tower, which was topped off by Johannes Hültz of Cologne in 1439 with a graceful lacy stone spire.

Most of the cathedral's hundreds of statues were destroyed during the French Revolution, but 67 were saved—many originals now finding sanctuary in the cathedral museum next door. The grand central porch was unharmed. It portrays Jesus' entry into Jerusalem, the Crucifixion and other Biblical scenes. Inside is a Flamboyant Gothic pulpit, as formidable as the preacher Geiler von Kaysersberg for whom it was built, famous for his fire-and-brimstone sermons against moral decay. Stained-glass windows (12th–14th centuries) in the nave and northern aisle include portraits of medieval German emperors. An astronomical clock (1838) provides a little "light relief" in the south arm of the transept. At midday (actually 12.30), figures of the apostles parade past Jesus, while a cock crows and flaps its wings.

STRASBOURG

Cathedral Square

On the corner of Rue Mercière, the venerable Pharmacie du Cerf dispensed ointments and medicine to the church's stone-masons and carpenters back in the 13th century; it's one of the oldest pharmacies in the country. Across the cathedral square is the handsome Maison Kammerzell (now a restaurant), its ground floor dating from 1467 and the sculpted wooden façade above it added in 1589.

Musée de l'Œuvre Notre-Dame

South of the cathedral on Place du Château, the museum exhibits the city's medieval and Renaissance art treasures in a beautifully preserved group of 14th-, 16th- and 17th-century houses surrounding a Gothic garden. The museum protects the more vulnerable statuary and stained glass from the cathedral as well as paintings by Konrad Witz, Martin Schongauer and Hans Baldung Grien.

Other Museums

Neighbouring Palais Rohan, the classical 18th-century residence of Strasbourg's cardinals and princes, strikes a distinctively French note in a historic centre that is otherwise so German in character. It houses the city's other important museums. The ground-floor Musée des Arts décoratifs boasts a magnificent collection of European porcelain and faïence, highlighting the startling craftsmanship of the town's Hannong family—note especially a huge turkey-shaped soup tureen. Furnished interiors compare lifestyles of Parisian and Alsatian aristocracy and bourgeois tastes in the 17th and 18th centuries.

The Musée des Beaux-Arts up on the first floor exhibits important works by Giotto, Botticelli and Raphael, as well as Hans Memling, Rubens, Van Dyck and Goya, with French paintings by Watteau, Delacroix and Courbet. The Musée de l'Art moderne includes Impressionists Manet, Renoir and Sisley and, among its 20th-century artists, Gustav Klimt and Strasbourg-born Jean (Hans) Arp and wife Sophie Taeuber-Arp. In the basement, the Archaeological Museum traces the region's history from 600,000 BC to AD 800 in artefacts, weapons, ceramics, jewellery and sculpture.

Across the Ill

On the far side of the Ill river lies a picturesque part of old Strasbourg, along the Quai des Bateliers and around the quaint 14th-century Place du Corbeau. Further along Quai Saint-Nicolas, the Musée Alsacien occupies a group of 16th- and 17th-century houses.

It harbours treasure-troves of ancient toys and dolls and other colourful pieces of Alsatian folklore, as well as ritual objects and other memorabilia of the region's Jewish community.

La Petite France

Strasbourg's most enchanting quarter, the old tannery district known as La Petite France, is at the west end of the city-centre island formed by canals and the Ill river. The tanners shared the waterways here with millers and fishermen. Along the Rue des Dentelles and the Rue du Bain-aux-Plantes, the sturdy gabled houses with their timbered façades and flower-bedecked balconies are splendid examples of 16th- and 17th-century German architecture.

A perfect place from which to view them—and the cathedral beyond—is the roof of the Barrage Vauban, part of the fortifications built by Sebastien Vauban for Louis XIV across the Ill after Strasbourg became French.

Palais de l'Europe

Guided tours (reservation is required) are available for Strasbourg's European institutions, the Council of Europe and the European Parliament when not in session or, on a limited basis and by written request, during debates. It was Winston Churchill who first suggested in 1942 that Strasbourg would be an appropriate site for such institutions, presently sharing the Palais de l'Europe. Representing over 600 million people, the Council debates educational, cultural, social and environmental questions, while the Parliament handles political affairs. Opened nearby in 1995, the striking Palais des Droits de l'Homme deals with concrete measures to respect the rights of the individual citizen.

Parc de l'Orangerie

Opposite the Palais d'Europe is the delightful Parc de l'Orangerie, designed in the 19th century. The garden pavilion was built in 1804; one of its frequent visitors was Napoleon's wife Josephine who liked to come and look at the flowers there. Among the park's pleasures are a waterfall and an artificial lake for boating. The Bürehiesel restaurant is a 17th-century Alsatian farmhouse which was transported here for an industrial fair in 1885.

Colmar

One of the most attractive towns in Alsace lies 16 km (10 miles) west of the Rhine and 68 km (42 miles) south of Strasbourg. This wine-trading centre is notable for its many fountains, Gothic churches and Renaissance houses, but above all for the magnificent

16th-century Isenheim Altarpiece by the German painter, Matthias Grünewald, housed in the Musée d'Unterlinden, formerly a convent.

The home of Frédéric-Auguste Bartholdi (1834–1904), sculptor of New York City's Statue of Liberty and Colmar-born, is now a museum.

Breisach

On the German bank, Breisach is strategically located and long a bone of contention in Franco-German wars. It is now best known for the art treasures in its Gothic cathedral (Münster). The carved wooden high altar (1526) of Mary's Coronation is signed only "HL" (identified by scholars as Hans Loi). Also here are Hans Baldung Grien's frescoes of the *Last Judgment* and the *Resurrection* (1488–91).

A tranquil corner of Strasbourg's Petite France.

Ottmarsheim

This small village on the French side of the river is little known but well worth visiting for its striking octagonal abbey church, founded in 1030 and designed on the model of the Palatine chapel in Aachen. It is not only the oldest church in Alsace, but also claims to be the oldest building. Two Gothic chapels were added, one on each side of the choir, in the 15th and 16th centuries. Most visitors, on entering the very understated chapel, are taken aback by its up-lifting beauty and harmony.

Basle

Switzerland's second biggest city (population close to 200,000, mostly German-speaking Protestant) is surrounded by fertile farmland, meadows, orchards, and the forests of the Jura mountains to the south. On the right bank of the river, Kleinbasel (Lesser Basle) is the town's industrial district, a skyline of smokestacks and construction cranes and the focus of its centuries-old international industrial fair. Most of the historical centre is concentrated on the left bank—Grossbasel (Greater Basle), with its twin Gothic towers, handsome medieval and Renaissance gabled houses, theatres and concert halls.

River View

For a first impression of the city's two facets, ancient and modern, go out to Mittlere Rheinbrücke, one of Basle's six bridges over the river. Upstream, the cathedral towers above a cluster of step-gabled medieval houses. Downstream, the pharmaceutical and chemical plants show you where the money comes from. Or, take one of the little ferryboats that ply their way across the river, not by smelly, noisy motor, but attached to an overhead cable and propelled merely by the stream from one bank to the other.

On the Kleinbasel right bank, you get a panoramic view of the historic skyline of Grossbasel. From the Mittlere Rheinbrücke, stroll along the Oberer Rheinweg riverside promenade, lined with imposing patrician houses of the 18th and 19th centuries. The house at No. 93 has a scale on its wall showing the various Rhine flood levels dating back to 1641.

Back on the left bank, notice at Schifflände 1, the Lällekeenig sculpture, a key figure in the traditional rivalry between the townsmen of Basle's two communities on either side of the river. The Grossbaslers' medieval king pokes his tongue out at the Kleinbaslers. The Kleinbaslers respond every January, on Vogel Gryff (Gryphon) Day, when a Kleinbasler dressed up as the Wilde Mann (savage) cavorts on the bridge with the Gryphon and the Lion in a scornful dance that culminates when he bares his bottom at the Lällekeenig. This ceremony launches the season of rumbustious jollity leading up to the Carnival (Fasnacht).

Münsterplatz

From the river, take a slow uphill walk to the town's lovely 18th-century square, where the Romans built their citadel. It is the site of the 12th-century Gothic Münster (cathedral). Restoration was carried out in the 19th century, respecting Romanesque elements, particularly in the apse,

that date from the first church built here in 1031. This massive fortress-like red sandstone edifice was the seat of prince-bishops who ruled the German imperial city with an iron hand until they were driven out in the Protestant Reformation in 1529.

The principal Gothic-arched porch between the towers is finely sculpted, but even more elegant, on the north side, is the Romanesque St Gallus Porch

---

WHEN BASLE BOUNCES

Hard-working Baslers have a certain reputation for restraint. After a stay here, German playwright Rolf Hochhuth said that, compared to Basle, the Englishman's famous understatement is downright megalomania. Well, that restraint goes out the window for Fasnacht. People launch into a three-day revel, dancing and piping their way through the streets in grotesque masks and gaudy costumes. The bars are full to bursting, the customers, too, day and night. And just to be different from other Rhineland carnivals, it all starts at 4 a.m. on the Monday morning following Ash Wednesday. Imagine: three working days when the burghers of Basle don't work.

with its rounded archway supported on slender columns flanking the tympanum of Jesus sitting in judgment over the door. In niches on either side of the arch are statues of Wise and Mad Virgins. Inside is an epitaph for the humanist philosopher Erasmus, who died here in 1536. The Pfalz terrace at the rear of the chancel, which is partly Romanesque, gives you a splendid view over the town, the swiftly flowing Rhine and beyond it, the Black Forest to the north and Vosges hills on the western horizon.

South of the Münster, the great modern Stadttheater rises above a multilevel plaza where the star attraction is Tinguely's mechanical fountain (1977), full of moving men playing and splashing in the water.

Old Town

The old city centre is now a pleasantly relaxed pedestrian zone. Stop for a coffee or beer on one of the café terraces on Barfüsserplatz before you follow two busy shopping streets, Falknerstrasse and Gerbergasse, that join up with Freie Strasse and converge on Marktplatz. The market is set up in the shadow of the imposing 16th-century late-Gothic and Renaissance Rathaus (town hall). Its decorative features include a gleaming gilded spire and handsome corbelled oriel win-

dows with a balcony at the top. The square clocktower with turrets at each corner is a modern addition.

Little has survived from the city's 14th-century fortifications, but the western gateway, Spalentor, with its clocktower, decoratively roofed gallery and crenellated watch towers, has been preserved. On the west side are pink sandstone sculptures of Mary and the prophets (15th century) and the city's coat of arms.

Kunstmuseum

At St Albangraben 16, the Art Museum is one of the most prestigious art institutions in Europe, the first to open to the general public—in 1661. Among its magnificent collection of 15th- and 16th-century German and Swiss paintings in the Gemäldegalerie are 15 paintings by Hans Holbein the Younger, who moved to Basle when an apprentice. His portraits of his wife and two children and Erasmus in old age are outstanding. Other masters include Grünewald, Martin Schongauer, Konrad Witz and Hans Baldung Grien. The modern collection is of the same high order: Picasso, Braque, Max Ernst, Klee and Kandinsky, and Americans Mark Rothko, Jasper Johns and Barnett Newman. There is also a department of Prints and Drawings (Kupferstichkabinett).

103

The Tinguely Museum, designed by Mario Botta, is just one of Basel's stunning avant-garde buildings.

Museum für Gegenwartskunst

More modern art, often at the very cutting edge of the avant-garde, is on display in the Museum of Contemporary Art, St Albantal 2. Here Joseph Beuys, Donald Judd and Frank Stella are housed in an old converted paper mill.

Haus zum Kirschgarten

For a glimpse of how the well-to-do Basle patrician lived in the 18th century, visit this mansion on Elisabethenstrasse 27, exhibiting the burghers' splendid furniture, chandeliers, clocks and monumental porcelain stoves.

Tinguely Museum

In Solitude Park on the right bank of the river, the building designed by Mario Botta houses a museum dedicated to the life and work of the kinetic artist Jean Tinguely (1925–91), with works in iron and scrap metal from the 1950s to the 80s.

Zoologischer Garten

Most zoos are out of favour in this ecologically sensitive age, but Basle's (600 different species of animal) is respected for being the first zoo in Europe where the rhinoceros and gorilla have reproduced in captivity. They, at least, were not too unhappy.

The River Neckar is justifiably considered one of Germany's most idyllic waterways. It rises at an altitude of 706 m (2,316 ft) in open country near the Swabian town of Villingen-Schwenningen. Over its 367-km (228-mile) length, it winds through the steep-sloped valleys of marine limestone on the edge of the Schwäbische Alb, cuts across broad valley meadows in the Stuttgart and Heilbronn basin to push through the Odenwald red sandstone and reach the Rhineland plain at Heidelberg. From there, it flows into the Rhine at Mannheim. On the way the Neckar is fed by several tributaries and becomes navigable after joining up with the River Fils at Plochingen, a few kilometres southeast of Stuttgart.

Right from prehistoric times, settlers have been drawn to the Neckar's richly varied country, broad fertile loops in the river and narrow, easily defended valley floors. They were above all interested in the Neckar Valley's natural resources: timber, sandstone, minerals, fish stocks and much coveted reserves of salt.

In the Middle Ages, many proud communities of knights and their castles sprang up along the river. Despite the region's turbulent history, most of these places have been able to retain their historical charm. Not the least of the Neckar Valley's is the fact that it counts among Germany's most important wine regions. This and the largely unspoiled countryside—above all in the area of the Neckar Valley and Odenwald Nature Park—have made the river and its hinterland a popular leisure and holiday destination.

Heidelberg

Heidelberg is Germany's oldest university town and one of the most charming. Beautifully situated amid the lush green woodlands of the Neckar Valley east of the Rhine, it has long been a contemplative home for philosophers and poets, a cradle of the German Romantic movement. There is certainly no more romantic ruin in Germany than Heidelberg's castle, for centuries the home of the Palatinate princes until burned out in the 17th century.

Scholars here have always drunk a lot, duelled a little and, when necessary, done an amazing amount of serious academic work. Among the most illustrious students and professors appear the poet Eichendorff, chemist Robert Bunsen (inventor of the

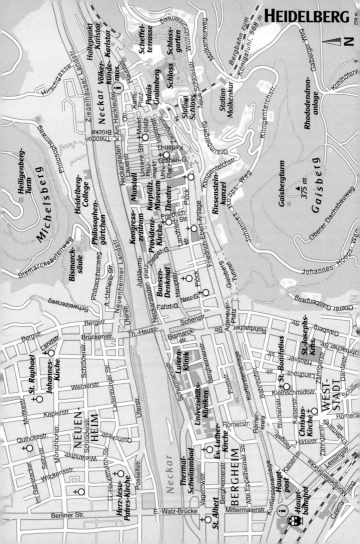

HEIDELBERG

famous Bunsen burner), philosophers G.W.F. Hegel and Karl Jaspers and sociologist Max Weber.

You may notice that several of the town's 18th-century baroque buildings have survived, but no more than one 16th-century Renaissance house. This is because, for once, the destruction was not the result of World War II bombs, but the ravages of Louis XIV's French troops in the 17th century. (The dastardly event is commemorated today with spectacular fireworks displays in summer.) Heidelberg was spared the region's bombardments of 1945 thanks to a particular American affinity for the place. In the 1920s, alumni of the university donated funds for new buildings. Some of them may well have been superiors in bomber command in 1945 when the city had already been singled out as headquarters for the US Army at the end of the war.

Philosophenweg

To capture the historic spirit of the university town and for a splendid view of the city itself nestling beneath the grand old castle, there's nowhere better to begin than the Philosophenweg (Philosopher's Path) on the north bank of the Neckar river. On your way up the Heiligenberg hillside to ruins of a Celtic refuge at the top, imagine Hegel plodding along, wondering how on earth he was going to get students to understand his theories of phenomenology, or Karl Jaspers grappling with transcendental existentialism. Did either find time to look at the lovely flowers in the gardens, one of them now named after the philosophers' favourite poet, Friedrich Hölderlin?

Take the winding Schlangenweg back down to the Karl-Theodor Bridge, where statues of this 18th-century Palatine prince (1724–99) are accompanied by allegorical figures representing the rivers that flowed through his territories (Rhine, Danube, Neckar and Mosel), and the Greek goddess Pallas Athena paying tribute to Karl-Theodor's patronage of the arts. He is further honoured at the east end of the city centre with the Karlstor, a baroque triumphal arch. Though it was meant to be merely decorative, the gate concealed three subterranean prison cells.

The Castle

A funicular railway gives you a spectacular introductory ride up to Heidelberg Castle, quite attractive in its ruined state. Turn left from the entrance through the Stückgarten. This is where the castle's heavy artillery pieces were mounted on the semi-circu- 107 lar Rondell tower, which offers a good view of the Neckar valley from the top. At the end of the garden you'll see the remains of the Dicker Turm (Fat Tower), originally 40 m (130 ft) tall with walls 7 m (23 ft) thick until they were blasted in half by French cannon.

The Elizabethpforte (1615), a triumphal arch, was built for Elizabeth Stuart, daughter of James I of England and wife of Palatinate prince Friedrich V. Across the moat is a dungeon with the ominous name of Seltenleer—"Seldom Empty".

Continue around the moat and across the bridge, defended by a domed gate-tower, to the main castle. In the summer, concerts and a theatre festival are held in the castle courtyard. To the right, in the Soldatenbau (Guards' quarters) with its projecting wellhouse in front, is the theatre ticket-office and a restaurant.

To the left is the Ruprechtsbau, begun in 1398 and completed 150 years later. On the upper left side of the façade, the prince's stone eagle holds in its claws the Palatine lion and Bavaria's distinctive emblem formed of lozenges. Inside, a monumental Renaissance sandstone fireplace dominates the Rittersaal (Knights' Hall).

The castle's most important building is the Ottheinrichsbau.

This landmark of German Renaissance architecture was built by Prince Otto Heinrich in 1559—the year of his death. It lost its gables in the French invasion, but the façade retains its decorative elegance with rich statuary around the windows and a triumphal arch doorway. Among the Biblical and mythological heroes portrayed, note David with sword and Goliath's head, Joshua with helmet, Samson with ass's jawbone and Hercules with cudgel. Otto Heinrich created here one of Europe's finest libraries. Some of the thousands of manuscripts carried away to the Vatican by Protestant Palatine's Catholic enemies in 1622 can now be consulted in microfilm form at Heidelberg's university library.

On the north side of the courtyard, the baroque façade of the Friedrichsbau (built in 1607 and restored in the 19th century) presents a gallery of rulers from Charlemagne in the upper left corner to the building's patron, Prince Friedrich IV.

Follow a ramp down to one of the castle's most popular attractions, the Fassbau (Barrel Wing), specially constructed to hold two gigantic wine barrels. The bigger one, built in 1751, could hold 221,726 litres, while the other (1662) had a capacity of a mere 45,000. The guardian of the barrels was a dwarf named Perkeo, ex-court-jester to the Medici in Florence. He was said to have drunk 10 to 12 litres of wine a day and lived to the age of 83—dying after drinking a glass of water. So say the local wine producers.

The Deutsches Apothekenmuseum (Pharmacy Museum) has its entrance in the castle courtyard under the staircase of the Ottheinrichsbau. Ten rooms trace the history of pharmacy and medical instruments over four centuries. Hypochondriacs will have a field day among the herbal chests, porcelain and crystal medicine jars, mortars, pestles, balances and retorts.

The Town

Something of the city centre's 17th-century atmosphere can be discerned on Marktplatz. Little shops and market stalls selling

books, souvenirs and trinkets still cling to the late-Gothic Heiliggeistkirche (Church of the Holy Ghost). Protestant iconoclasts deprived the church of almost all its sculptural and other ornament, then, in 1693, French looters left the chancel bare save for the 15th-century carved tombstone of Prince-elector Ruprecht III and his wife Elisabeth.

At Hauptstrasse 178, opposite the church, the late-Renaissance Haus zum Ritter (House of the Knight), with pink sandstone ornament, was the only private house to survive the French army's fires. Lofty and sturdily built, it is guarded by a statue of St George on the gable. The owner, merchant Charles Bélier,

Seen from above or from street level, Heidelberg oozes charm.

was a Huguenot refugee from France. He was evidently more broad-minded than his Calvinist brethren: to the gable inscription, *Soli Deo Gloria* (Glory is God's Alone), he added, lower down, the less pious *Persta In Invicta Venus* (May Venus Endure Unconquered).

There are several interesting baroque buildings on Hauptstrasse. Haus zum Riesen at No. 52 was built in 1708 with masonry recycled from the castle's Dicker Turm. The 18th-century Palais Morass, No. 97, houses the Kurpfälzisches Museum. Its collections of Gothic and Renaissance painting and sculpture include a magnificent group carved by Tilman Riemenschneider, the Twelve Apostles Altar (Zwölfbotenaltar). Among the 19th- and 20th-century paintings are works by the Heidelberg Romantics and German Expressionists Karl Schmidt-Rottluff, Max Slevogt and Emil Nolde.

Founded in 1386, the University, on Universitätsplatz and Augustinergasse, is the most ancient in Germany, though the oldest buildings here date back only to 1712. Students used to be jailed in the Karzer, Augustinergasse 2, where visitors can contemplate the rascals' black silhouette portraits and insolent graffiti. Across the river, the university's Museum of Geology and Palaeontology, Im Neuenheimer Feld 234, reconstitutes 2 billion years of earth history. The highlight is the lower jaw of *Homo heidelbergensis*, 600,000 years old.

Along the River

The start of the river cruise could not be more beautiful: immediately beyond Heidelberg comes the romantic wilderness of the Neckar Valley-Odenwald Nature Park. This unique reserve is fascinating for its diversity, a paradise for ramblers and naturelovers. On the lower Neckar, there are also several enchanting small medieval towns: Neckargemünd, Neckarsteinach, Hirschhorn and Eberbach, known as the "Romantic Quartet" on the European Burgenstrasse (Castle Route) extending from Mannheim to Prague.

Neckargemünd

It is just 10 km (6 miles) upriver to "Heidelberg's beautiful neighbour". The thousand-year-old town with its old city-walls and half-timbered gabled houses was once in earlier years an important logistical crossroads on military routes. Still very impressive are the ruins of the 11th–12th century mountain fortress of Filsberg towering over the town.

Diagonally opposite on the other side of the river is the invitingly peaceful presence of

Neckarsteinach, the "town of four castles". The four fortresses (two of them still inhabited) were built between the 11th and 13th centuries by the noble freemen of Steinach. Best known representative of this aristocratic clan was Bligger II (1152–1210), gifted poet, minstrel and reputed by some scholars to have authored the Song of the Nibelungen that inspired Richard Wagner's opera cycle.

Hirschhorn

A few kilometres further on, the Neckar forms a double loop curving between the densely wooded slopes of the Odenwald. In the middle is the town of Hirschhorn, which bears the proud title of "Pearl of the Neckar Valley". The fortified medieval town lies beneath a former Carmelite monastery and the jutting towers of the castle built by the barons of Hirschhorn. A Renaissance palace was added to the castle in the 16th century and has been transformed now into a luxury hotel.

Eberbach

The old Staufer stronghold and former Imperial city of Eberbach offers its visitors a splendid array of patrician houses, massive defensive walls and towers, handsomely restored medieval quarters and highly reputed mineral springs. In the Thalheimsches Haus (1390) near the old powder magazine is the in-

formation centre for the Neckar Valley-Odenwald Nature Park. The Eberbacher Museum is well worth a visit for its exhibits about the region, its history, geology and the story of the Neckar's river traffic.

Feudal Castles
The next part of the journey takes you through a region that was already inhabited in prehistoric times and remarkable for the beauty of its landscape and mighty feudal castles. The river is bordered by towpaths that were once used for pulling freight barges upstream.

Burg Zwingenberg is known for the annual summer opera and music festival staged in the castle grounds. Behind the fortress, the

Bad Wimpfen is known for its picturesque skyline.

Wolfschlucht ("wolf ravine") behind the fortress inspired some of the scenes Carl Maria von Weber wrote for his opera, *Der Freischütz*.

Behind the old village of Neckargerach with its romantic 12th-century Minneburg, you pass the narrow Margarethen-schlucht that marks the the actual end of the Odenwald. This is where the first vineyards begin.

Next to welcome you are Schloss Neuburg, begun near Obrigheim in the 10th century, and the 11th-century Burg Hornberg, part of which is now a hotel, near Neckarzimmern. Its most famous resident was the 16th-century knight, Götz von Berlichingen, the title character of Goethe's tragedy.

Burg Guttenberg

Well worth a side-trip is this mighty castle from the Staufer era. As the buildings were constantly extended but never destroyed, you can take in the whole structural development of the medieval fortifications. The fascinating castle museum has a wealth of historical and artistic treasures. Guttenberg is also the seat of the Deutsche Greifenwarte, an agency for protecting birds of prey, above all rearing the white-tailed sea eagle.

On the other bank is Gundelsheim, a town founded by the Teutonic Order *(Deutschordenstadt)*, with the Teutonic Master living in its 15th-century Burg Horneck.

Bad Wimpfen

The Staufers' former imperial court, Bad Wimpfen is one of Germany's most charming little towns. Down in the valley, the older part, Wimpfen im Tal, is of Roman origin. It is Wimpfen am Berg up on the hill that has the famous medieval skyline. It owes this mainly to Emperor Friedrich II, though his grandfather Friedrich Barbarossa did hold an imperial council here in 1182. The most notable surviving buildings are the Roter Turm (red tower); a double-arcaded wall of the old palace; the Steinhaus, Germany's biggest Romanesque dwelling, (now housing the Historical Museum); the Blauer Turm (blue tower); and the Stadtkirche, with a late-Gothic nave added on.

The castle district's narrow lanes are lined with historic houses from different periods, providing a perfect setting for traditional festivals and markets. Down in Wimpfen im Tal, the church of St Peter (Ritterstiftskirche) is an early-Gothic masterpiece that belong now to the Benedictine abbey of Grüssau.

Bad Wimpfen's spa, popular for its brine baths, is located on the north side of town. Bad Wimpfen actually owes its emergence as a spa resort to neighbouring Bad Friedrichshall where most of the brine and salt originate. The Kochendorf Salt Mine makes an impressive visit.

Neckarsulm

The old Frankish settlement of Neckarsulm, today a wine town and a manufacturing centre for Audi cars, was once a town of the Teutonic Order (1484–1805). The castle now houses the Zweirad- und NSU-Museum (two-wheeled vehicles and vintage cars).

Heilbronn

Beyond Neckarsulm, the river divides into two arms as it flow through the centre of Heilbronn. Nestling among vineyards, the modern industrial and commercial centre was almost completely destroyed in World War II, but has been rebuilt along with its historical monuments.

Heilbronn's landmark is the Kilianskirche with its stone-lanterned tower. In the Gothic interior is Hans Seyfer's magnificent high altar (1498). The 62-m (203-ft) tower is said to be the first Renaissance structure built north of the Alps. On the tip, the infantryman known as *Männle* is a copy; its original stands in the Rathaus arcade. The Rathaus (town hall) on Marktplatz was built in several different styles, its jewel being the astronomic clock (1580) above the porch. In the hall of honour is a memorial to Heilbronn's 11,000 casualties in World War II. East of Marktplatz, is the 43-m (141-ft) Hafenmarktturm, once part of a monastery.

From the pedestrian zone south to the river bank, you reach the Deutschordensmünster (Minster of the Teutonic Order) and the Deutschhof (Teutonic Court, begun in the 13th century) which house a cultural centre and sculpture museum. The Historical Museum is located in the nearby Fleisch- und Gerichtshaus (Meat hall and Courthouse, 1598). In front is a statue of Käthchen von Heilbronn, a sleepwalking girl who inspired a play of the same name by Heinrich von Kleist.

Ludwigsburg

A short distance beyond Heilbronn, the river forms another broad loop before the towns come closer together on the banks and you reach the baroque town of Ludwigsburg.

Originally in 1704, Württemberg's Duke Eberhard Ludwig wanted just to rebuild his hunting lodge here, but by 1733 it had grown into the "Swabian Versailles", a splendid palace with 452 richly decorated rooms in 18 buildings. On a guided tour, you can also see the porcelain collection from the Ludwigsburger

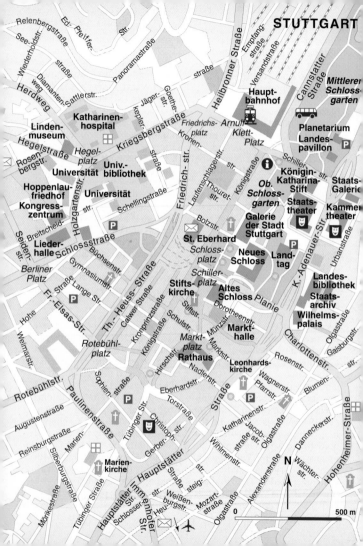

Manufaktur (factory, founded in 1758). Just as imposing as the palace are the vast gardens, each with its own botanical theme. Every year from Easter to October, the "Blühendes Barock" (Baroque in Bloom) show turns the garden into a sea of flowers.

Behind the main palace in a deer park is the pretty Jagd- und Lustschloss Favorite ("Favorite" Hunting Lodge, 1713–23), built for the Duke's mistress Wilhelmina von Gravenitz. Further out is the Seeschloss Monrepos, an exquisite rococo lake pavilion reflected in the waters.

West of the palace, the Ludwigsburg town centre has an enchanting arcaded market square, two baroque churches and attractive shops and cafés.

Just a few kilometres on is Baden-Württemberg's capital, Stuttgart (population: 591,284).

Stuttgart

From the main railway station, built in the modern International Style in 1927, Königsstrasse leads to the historic town centre. After the Kunstgebäude (1910) housing the Stadtgalerie, devoted principally to German art from 19th century to the present day, you reach the Neues Schloss (1746–1807) which the regional government uses for official receptions. The neighbouring Altes Schloss, originally a 13th-century moated castle, has gone through various expansions and alterations. Today it is the seat of the Württembergisches Landesmuseum telling the region's story with art and artefacts from prehistory to the present. Take a look, too, at the pretty palace church. Opposite is Stuttgart's landmark, the asymmetric towers of the Stiftskirche, a collegiate church from the time of the Staufers (1170). Inside are the princes' tombs of the Württemberg dynasty.

Further along Königsstrasse, the modern Rathaus has a carillon on its 60-m (197-ft) tower playing Swabian folk tunes. Off to the right is the Calwer Passage with its fashionable shops and restaurants.

One of the town's top attractions is the Staatsgalerie west of the Hauptbahnhof. The neoclassical building houses works from the Middle Ages to the 19th century. The striking modern building by the great British architect James Stirling is devoted to modern art.

The philosopher Georg Wilhelm Friedrich Hegel was born in Stuttgart in 1770; you can visit his birthplace, the Hegel-Haus, Eberhardstrasse 53.

For a view over the city and the Neckar Valley, go to Stuttgart-Degerloch and its Fernsehturm (TV tower) with an observation deck 150 m (492 ft) up.

Shopping

On this journey through four countries—five, if you go into Lux-embourg—you will have a wealth of opportunities for shopping; high quality goods range from antiques to fine wines.

The Netherlands

Dutch cigars are renowned the world over for their aroma. Diamonds are a speciality in a Amsterdam, with a well-deserved reputation for their cutting and polishing. Silver and pewter provide any number of useful or decorative gifts from bracelets to ashtrays. Delft and Makkum china is delicate and distinctively different. In the souvenir shops you'll find clogs of all sizes, to hang on a keyring or use as a planter; tea, spices, bottles, candles, bamboo basketwork; dozens of colourful keepsakes. You could also buy some tulip bulbs, but check with customs regulations in your country as some refuse the import of plants. Dutch gin, *Jenever*, has a special taste. Made with juniper berries, it is less fiery than English gin.

Germany

In high fashion, Düsseldorf designers have made an international reputation, but most of the labels you will see here in the major towns are French, Italian, Japanese and American. Leather and sports wear are good quality, especially for hunting and hiking.

One luxury item in the realm of haute couture was created in the Rhineland, still available in its original form in its famous green-labelled bottle, Eau de Cologne. When first produced in 1709 by Johann Maria Farina, it was known as *Aqua Mirabilis* (Wonderful Water). It got its French name during the Napoleonic Occupation and switched to *Kölnisch Wasser* during the nationalist 19th century.

Fine china is a German speciality. Besides traditional Meissen and modern designs of Rosenthal, the best-known regional manufacture is from Frankenthal, near Mannheim, sometimes reproducing great rococo pieces from its 18th century heyday. As a luxury china toy for children (or their parents), look out for exquisite dolls' tea services in copies of Meissen and Frankenthal classics.

For sheer workmanship, Germany's toys are a delight, its electric trains still the world's best. Others swear by the model aircraft, boats and spaceships. With construction kits, build your own medieval castle or Cologne cathedral. Dolls in traditional costume are of superb quality, as are teddy bears and other cuddly creatures.

Bed and table linens are also an old tradition. The German duck- or goosedown Federbett quilt or duvet is a lifetime investment. Beside the warm-as-toast winter model, there is the lightweight model for summer. Knowledgeable campers go for the great sleeping-bags.

Musical instruments in the land of Beethoven and Brahms range from the finest harmonica to a great grand piano. Germany has made a comeback in the camera market, with art-photographers and spies still going for the Leica and Minox. Miniature but powerful binoculars are great inside cathedrals and castles, to get a close-up of remote details.

In Frankfurt, book lovers would do well to browse the area surrounding the Goethehaus or Hauptwache, or, for second-hand and antiquarian books, near the Römer and cathedral.

Among gourmet delicacies, top choice, of course, is the Rhine

An ephemeral souvenir from Holland—you can also buy bulbs.

and Mosel wine, which vineyards will ship for you, though you may prefer to carry your own bottle of Schnaps. Delicatessens will also gift-wrap locally made salami sausage and hams. In the pastry shops, your best bets for long-distance travel are Lebkuchen (gingerbread) and marzipan in all shapes and sizes.

Luxembourg

Delicately decorated porcelain by the world-renowned Luxembourg firm Villeroy et Boch, as well as crystal, will make a superb table setting fit for a Grand Duchess.

Since they are difficult to buy outside the country, consider a bottle or two of Luxembourg wine, fruit-based liqueurs or brandies—mirabelle, plum, pear, cherry, apple, blackcurrant and walnut are the best flavours; *lie* is distilled from the residue after wine-making.

France

Among the gourmet delicacies of Alsace, *pâté de foie gras* is sold in charming earthenware pots you will want to keep long after you've finished the pâté. Big tins of *choucroute (sauerkraut)*, complete with sausages and hams, are ready to be re-heated. Wines are a good buy, available in gift packs of three, six or more bottles. The local *eaux-de-vie* also make welcome presents, notably kirsch or mirabelle. For old Alsatian furniture and other bric-a-brac, try the flea market *(brocante)* every Wednesday and Saturday on Place du Vieil-Hôpital. Rare second-hand books and manuscripts are sold at the book market, appropriately on and around Place Gutenberg (Tuesday, Wednesday and Saturday).

Switzerland

In Basle, traditional carnival masks can be found second-hand or new at the flea markets on Petersplatz and Barfüsserplatz. As for wristwatches, the plastic Swatch in all its dazzling variety has not ousted the hand-made pieces that make precision instruments a work of art. Priced in between is a splendid miniaturized version of the Swiss railway-platform clock. A Swiss Army pocket knife, with all its accessory gadgets from fish scaler and cigar-cutter to toothpick, can make a dinner guest the hero of the day by whipping it out to use the corkscrew for the wine when the host has mislaid his own. It comes in traditional red and elegant silver. (Don't put it into your hand luggage.) In all the local pastry shops and confectioners you will see smart white packets of Leckerli—a small chewy, spicy biscuit flavoured with cinnamon, cloves and citrus peel.

Dining Out

Rhinelanders have a robust appetite for the good life. Portions are generous, and while beer remains the favourite thirst-quencher, the local wines are to be sipped and savoured.

It is difficult to put your finger on what really constitutes Dutch cuisine. In general, main dishes are meat oriented and of a consistently high standard.

Apart from snacks and cakes, what the Dutch really seem to enjoy are herring fillets, which they down at street stalls in one fell gulp. Try *kroket*, spiced meat in breadcrumbs, or a *pannekoek* with any number of possible fillings. *Poffertjes* are extremely substantial little pancakes served with powdered sugar and butter, while other delicious temptations include *oliebollen*, a type of fruit doughnut, and waffles smothered in syrup.

For those who prefer something spicier, the Netherlands can call on its colonial connections with Indonesia and Surinam to provide opportunities for a taste of the exotic. Indonesian restaurants can be found in every town. A particular highlight is *rijsttafel*, rice or noodles with more than a dozen very tasty meat, fish and vegetable side dishes and accompanied by a hot sambal sauce.

As for drinks, Dutch beers rarely disappoint. Regional specialities include *witbieren* (white beers), which, served with a slice of lemon, are very refreshing. Try *jenever*, a type of Dutch schnaps made from juniper and molasses and served in tiny glasses as either *oude* (old) or *jonge* (young), plain, lemon- or blackcurrant-flavoured.

In Germany, you will often find the staple dishes—soups, stews and roasts, sausages and *sauerkraut*, roast pork or fish—mixing sweet and sour, with fruit and vegetables on the same plate. After hearty lentil and bean soups in winter, summer menus may propose cold fruit-soup (*Fruchtsuppe*) made with cherries, strawberries or red currants, set off with a little lemon juice.

Menus in the Rhineland reflect the local sense of humour. In this Catholic heartland, a dish of spicy black blood sausage (*Blutwurst*) served on top of stewed apples and boiled potatoes is known as *Himmel und Erde* (heaven and earth). Similarly, the Cologne speciality of blood sausage with slices of raw onion is called *Kölscher Kaviar*. On the other hand, there is no joke about the nationally revered *Sauerbraten*, sweet and sour beef cooked in red wine with currants, onions, gingerbread and pepper and served with potato dumplings *(Kartoffelklösse)*. One of the beneficial legacies of the French occupation of the Rhineland is the *Chaudeau*, a soufflé with sultanas, white wine and cinnamon, but nobody needed French chefs to show them how to make the delicious *Worbelekoche* blueberry cake.

Frankfurt's food and wine district is known as the *Fressgasse*, which means, roughly,

"eating trough". Apart from the justly famed *Frankfurter* sausage, local favourites include game, particularly venison and boar, and *Rippchen* (smoked pork chops) with sauerkraut. In the earthy taverns of Sachsenhausen, try the local apple-wine *(Ebbelwoi)* with *Handkäs mit Musik*, a ripe cheese with "music", in fact a salad of finely sliced onions served with black bread.

Every region of France has its own special cuisine. Strasbourg claims to have invented *pâté de foie gras*, just before the French Revolution. Goose braised with apples *(oie braisée aux pommes)* or simply roasted and served on red or white cabbage is a gourmet's delight. The local version of sauerkraut, *choucroute,* is testimony to Franco-German cooperation:

You're not likely to go hungry in Germany or Alsace!

pickled cabbage, simmered in Alsatian Riesling and juniper berries, adding a glass of kirsch before crowning it with Alsatian ham, sausage and salt pork. For fish-lovers, *matelote* is the Alsatian freshwater answer to Mediterranean *bouillabaisse*, combining in one huge pot pike, eel, perch, tench and burbot, again cooked in a Riesling white wine.

The best local cheese, according to connoisseurs, is the very pungent Munster.

Marvellous fruit tarts include blueberry *(myrtilles)*, damson *(quetsches)* and yellow cherry-plum *(mirabelles)*.

Basle's culinary specialities include *Basler Mehlsuppe* (Basle flour soup), a hearty and much more tasty starter than it sounds, thanks to the addition of herbs and seasoning. The *Klöpfer* is Basle's version of the smoked cervelas sausage made from pork and beef, one of 48 different Swiss sausages you may find in salads, hors d'oeuvres platters or as a main dish.

Among freshwater fish from the surrounding lakes: *Egli* (perch) and *Forelle* (trout). Delicious accompaniments are *Rösti*, hashed potato cake, and *Spätzli*, noodle-like dumplings.

Two local pastries are *Basler Leckerli* gingerbread with honey and almond, and *Kirschtorte* cake laced with Kirsch.

Wines

The top Rhine wines come from the Rheingau around Rüdesheim. The late-harvested Riesling grape constitutes 80 per cent of the crop, producing a fine, fruity, mellow wine. The most prestigious labels are Schloss Johannisberger, Hattenheimer, Kloster Eberbacher, Rüdesheimer and Steinberger. The best of the increasingly popular reds come from Assmannshausen and Ingelheim. Besides the ever-popular Liebfraumilch, the Rheinhessen region south of Mainz is famous for the great Niersteiner Domtal and Oppenheim. The Rheinpfalz (Rhineland Palatinate) is understandably proud of its Deidesheimer and Wachenheimer.

The green-bottled Mosel wines (as opposed to brown-bottled Rhine wines) are reputed for their delicacy, the most celebrated being the Bernkasteler, Piesporter, Graacher and Zeltinger.

Alsace classes its white wines by the three main grapes used in production: *Riesling*, elegantly blending sweet and acid, ideal with fish and choucroute; aromatic *Gewürztraminer*, dry or fruity, fine for foie gras, meats and game; and light *Sylvaner*, a versatile table wine that goes perfectly with seafood, sausage and choucroute.

Switzerland also produces excellent wines, well worth trying.

The Hard Facts

To plan your trip, here are some of the practical details you should know about the lands along the Rhine:

Climate

The Rhineland is blessed with a relatively mild climate all year round, but the best months to visit are from April to October. Though the Rhine river in its southern reaches and the Mosel Valley are slightly warmer, you will always need a raincoat for surprise showers and sweater for cool evenings, even in summer. Average temperatures rise from 16°C (61°F) in April to 25°C (77°F) in July, declining again to 14°C (57°F) in October. January is the coldest month—3°C (37°F). Autumn is the most beautiful time at the heart of the Rhine Valley when the trees and vineyards turn to red and gold.

Communications

Call worldwide with telecards from street phones, much cheaper than the hotel's surcharge service. International dialling code to the Netherlands is 31, Germany 49, France 33, and Switzerland 41.

Customs controls

For the Netherlands, Germany, France and Luxembourg, customs controls are minimal at point of entry, with an official import allowance duty-free of 200 cigarettes or 50 cigars or 250 g tobacco and 1 litre of spirits plus 4 litres of wine for passengers from outside the EU aged 17 and over.

For Switzerland, residents of European countries may import 200 cigarettes or 50 cigars or 250 g tobacco (twice that amount for residents of non-European countries), and all passengers can import 2 litres of alcoholic beverages up to 15° and 1 litre over 15°, and a maximum of 20 litres of wine subject to payment of duty.

Emergencies

The standard emergency phone number is 112. Consular help is there only for critical situations, lost passports or worse, not for lost cash or travel tickets.

Essentials

Pack very little. In any case, clothing should be light—in summer, cottons are less sticky than synthetics. In these days of global warming, remember to pack sunblock, a sun hat, but also that sweater for cool evenings. Good walking shoes are important for excursions through the vineyards. Include insect-repellent and a pocket torch (flashlight).

Formalities

You will need a valid passport or an identity card. No special health certificates are required for European or North American citizens.

Health

There is a reciprocal health care agreement between EU countries: before leaving home, obtain a European Health Card (which has replaced the E111 form). Travellers from countries outside the EU should check that their medical insurance is valid in Europe. Doctors, dentists and hospital staff are of generally good standard, many speaking English. If you anticipate need of prescription medicines, take your own as you may not find the exact equivalent on the spot. Note that Switzerland is not in the EU.

Money

The euro is the official currency in all the countries mentioned here except Switzerland, where it is accepted in many shops and restaurants (but in notes or by credit card only). The Swiss Franc (CHF) is divided into 100 Rappen or centimes. Banknotes are issued in denominations of 10, 20, 50, 100, 200 and 1000 francs; coins of 5, 10, 20, 50 centimes, 1, 2 and 5 francs.

Photography

Most museums allow cameras, but ask permission; the same goes for taking photos of people. Do not photograph military installations.

Public Holidays

Netherlands:

January 1	*New Year's Day*
April 30	*Queen's Birthday*
Dec. 25	*Christmas Day*
Dec. 26	*Boxing Day*

Moveable: Good Friday, Easter Monday, Ascension Day, Whit Monday

Germany:

January 1	*New Year's Day*
May 1	*Labour Day*
August 15	*Assumption*
October 3	*German Unification*
Nov. 1	*All Saints Day*
Dec. 25	*Christmas Day*
Dec. 26	*Boxing Day*

Moveable: Good Friday, Easter Monday, Ascension Day, Whit Monday, Corpus Christi

Luxembourg:

January 1	*New Year's Day*
May 1	*Labour Day*
June 23	*National Day*
Nov. 1	*All Saints Day*
Dec. 25	*Christmas Day*

Dec. 26   *Boxing Day*
Moveable: Easter Monday,
Ascension Day, Whit Monday

France:
January 1   *New Year's Day*
May 1   *Labour Day*
May 8   *1945 Victory Day*
July 14   *Bastille Day*
August 15   *Assumption*
Nov. 1   *All Saints Day*
Nov. 11   *Remembrance Day*
Dec. 25   *Christmas Day*
Moveable: Easter Monday,
Ascension Day, Whit Monday

Switzerland:
January 1   *New Year's Day*
August 1   *National Day*
Dec. 25   *Christmas Day*
Moveable: Good Friday, Easter
Monday, Ascension Day, Whit
Monday

Safety

In large towns, pickpockets may
be prevalent in crowded places.
Without undue paranoia, don't
tempt them with an open handbag
or a wallet in the hip pocket.
Leave passports and valuables in
the purser's safe.

Social graces

You will generally find that the
people you meet are friendly and
polite. In Germany, they tend to
shake hands rather than give a
Latin hug. Everyone will be
pleasantly surprised to hear you
greet them with a couple of
words in their language. A *Guten
Tag* (good morning) or *Guten
Abend* (good evening), *Bitte*
(please), *Danke* (thanks), *Bitte
schön* (don't mention it) and *Auf
Wiedersehen* are always welcome, as are a *bonjour, s'il vous
plaît, merci* and *au revoir*. And
however casually dressed or
underdressed you might be for
the bar or café, remember to dress
decently when entering a church.

Tipping

Service is included in restaurant
and hotel bills, shared among the
whole staff, but an extra 5 or 10%
is customary. Be careful when
paying by credit card to fill in the
"Total" line, sometimes left blank
for you to add, if you wish, an
extra tip.

Toilets

When a little male or female
figure does not indicate which is
which, you should know that the
women's room is usually sign-
posted *Damen/Dames* and the
men's by *Herren/Hommes*. Public toilets are usually immaculate,
but if you use the facilities in a
bar or restaurant, it is customary
to order at least a drink there.

Voltage

Electric current is 220-volt 50-
cycle A.C.; take adaptors for any
sensitive electronic equipment.

INDEX

INDEX

GENERAL EDITOR: Barbara Ender-Jones
LAYOUT: Luc Malherbe
MAPS: JPM Publications; Elsner & Schichor; Huber Kartographie
PHOTO CREDITS: Bildagentur Huber: front cover, inside front cover, pp. 16, 44, 47, 49, 60, 64, 87, 88–89, 122; Hémisphères/Wysocki: back cover, pp. 22, 99, 109; D. Michellod: pp. 1, 80; CORBIS: pp. 2, 10, 36, 70, 119; Rheinland-Pfalz Tourismus GmbH: p. 4; Tourist-Information Trier: pp. 6, 52; www.koblenz-bilder.de: p. 14–15; www.düsseldorf.de: p. 32; Mairie de Metz/Christian Legay Marc Roger: p. 59; stadt.mainz: p. 69; www.frankfurt.de: p. 74; www.aschaffenburg.de: p. 77; K. Hoffmann/www.speyer.de: p. 90; Musée Tinguely, Christian Baur, Basel: p. 104; Tourist-Information Bad Wimpfen: pp. 112–113

Printed in Switzerland — Weber/Bienne (CTP) — 05/01/01 — Edition 2005